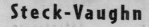

Steck-Vaughn

Reading Comprehension

Building Vocabulary and Meaning

Teacher's Guide

LEVEL
B

Reviewers

Lee Waggener

Second Grade Teacher
Bon View Elementary
Ontario-Montclair School District
Ontario, California

Argen Hurley

First Grade Teacher
Ballast Point Elementary
Hillsborough County School District
Tampa, Florida

STECK-VAUGHN

A Harcourt Company

www.steck-vaughn.com

Contents

Graphic Organizer Transparencies
Main Idea and Details Chart, Summary Web, Plot Chart, Author's Purpose Chart, Prediction Chart, Venn Diagram, Setting Chart, Fact-and-Opinion Chart, Realism-and-Fantasy Chart, Cause-and-Effect Chart, Drawing Conclusions Chart, Sequence Chart

"Comprehension is the reason for reading."

(Armbruster, Lehr, & Osborn, 2001)

While this statement might seem obvious, it is the premise for *Steck-Vaughn Reading Comprehension: Building Vocabulary and Meaning.* Readers who understand what they read are good readers. Current research has identified what good readers do when they read. It has also shown that students can learn the strategies and processes of good readers—and that this improves their overall comprehension of text. *Steck-Vaughn Reading Comprehension: Building Vocabulary and Meaning* provides explicit instruction and practice in the strategies that good readers use.

"Comprehension is critically important to development of children's reading skills and therefore their ability to obtain an education."

(National Reading Panel, 2000)

To develop students' reading comprehension, *Steck-Vaughn Reading Comprehension: Building Vocabulary and Meaning* offers both a model of comprehension instruction and supportive context for instruction. Specifically, this series provides students with the following key elements:

- **Experience reading different genres.** Each student book includes a variety of fiction and nonfiction genres, such as folktales, historical fiction, science articles, and persuasive essays.

- **Opportunities for reading and rereading.** Each lesson includes a four-page reading selection that allows students to practice and apply skills, strategies, and knowledge. Specific tips in the Teacher's Guide offer help in promoting students' reading fluency.

- **Explicit instruction.** Each student lesson defines a focus comprehension skill and instructs students on how to use it. Tips placed at point-of-use provide suggestions that help students use the skill as they read.

- **Vocabulary and concept development through experience, reading, and discussion.** Each lesson taps into students' prior knowledge about the lesson's topic. Then the lesson develops their concept vocabulary through prereading discussion. Point-of-use placement of the vocabulary word definitions and a follow-up Vocabulary activity help students build and extend their vocabulary. Students can also use the Glossary to reference definitions and pronunciations of content vocabulary.

- **Teacher modeling use of the skill.** Students and teacher work through the skill as a group, using appropriate graphic organizers, which are provided on transparencies.

- **Meaningful discussion about text.** Students engage in thinking and discussion about the text on literal and higher, more inferential levels.

- **Guided practice followed by independent use of the comprehension skill.** Each lesson provides guided practice of the comprehension skill.

- **Experience writing different genres.** Each lesson gives students an opportunity to plan and write a personal response based on the genre of the selection, which reinforces connections between reading and writing.

- **Review of the comprehension skills.** Review pages after every six lessons help students maintain skills learned.

- **Standardized test practice.** Test formats that students will encounter on standardized tests are used on the Comprehension, Vocabulary, and Review pages.

Steck-Vaughn Reading Comprehension: Building Vocabulary and Meaning supports practices outlined in the National Reading Panel report, aligns with the International Reading Association (IRA) and National Council of Teachers of English (NCTE) Standards for the English Language Arts, and helps students achieve state and national literacy standards. The teaching framework of *Reading Comprehension: Building Vocabulary and Meaning* encompasses critical strategies for developing reading and writing skills.

Literacy Goals	Research Says:	Reading Comprehension: Building Vocabulary and Meaning Suggests:
Text Comprehension Comprehension allows students to read, understand, and critique text in a meaningful and productive way.	• "Comprehension instruction can effectively motivate and teach readers to learn and use comprehension strategies that benefit the reader." (National Reading Panel, 2000) • "Good comprehension instruction includes both explicit instruction in specific comprehension strategies and a great deal of time and opportunity for actual reading, writing, and discussion of text." (Duke & Pearson, 2002)	specific comprehension strategies that guide students to be aware of how well they are comprehending as they read and write.
Vocabulary Vocabulary knowledge is fundamental to reading comprehension as students cannot comprehend text without knowing what most of the words mean.	• "Vocabulary learning is effective when it entails active engagement in learning tasks." (National Reading Panel, 2000) • "To improve reading comprehension, children need rich, in-depth knowledge of words." (Nagy, 2000)	teaching strategies that include vocabulary instruction before, during, and after reading.
Fluency Fluency is the ability to read a text with speed and accuracy, which provides a bridge between word recognition and comprehension.	• "Frequent opportunities to practice identifying words through meaningful reading and writing experiences help the reader to achieve automatic word identification or automaticity." (Worthy & Broaddus, 2002)	opportunities for both oral reading and independent reading.
Writing Writing is an integral part of the comprehension process, as it is essential that students connect reading to writing.	• "Students should experience writing the range of genres we wish them to comprehend. Their instruction should emphasize connections between reading and writing." (Duke & Pearson, 2002)	independent prewriting with the use of graphic organizers and writing prompts that inspire a personal response.
Language Development Language development skills focus on students' communication skills by exploring and developing vocabulary.	• "Print exposes children to words outside their vocabulary far more effectively than conversational talk or other media like watching television." (Cunningham & Stanovich, 1998) • "Pairing books of fact and fiction allows students to become familiar with selected topics and vocabulary." (Camp, 2000)	print-rich environments in both fiction and nonfiction that provide opportunities and tools for developing language.

REFERENCES

Armbruster, B.B., Lehr, F., & Osborn, J. (2001). *Put reading first: The research building blocks for teaching children to read.* Washington, DC: National Institute for Literacy.

Camp, D. (2000). It takes two: Teaching with twin texts of fact and fiction. *The Reading Teacher, 53*(5) 400–408.

Cunningham, A.E., & Stanovich, K. (1998). What reading does for the mind. *American Educator, 22,* 8–15.

Duke, N.K., & Pearson, D. (2002). Effective practices for developing reading comprehension. Farstrup, A.E., & Samuels, S.J. (Eds.) *What research has to say about reading instruction* (4th ed., pp. 205–242). Newark, DE: International Reading Association.

Nagy, W.E. (2000). *Teaching vocabulary to improve reading comprehension.* Urbana, IL: National Council of Teachers of English and Newark, DE: International Reading Association. (ERIC Document Reproduction No. ED298471)

National Reading Panel. (2000). *Teaching children to read: An evidence-based assessment of the scientific research literature on reading and its implications for reading instruction. Reports of the subgroups.* Bethesda, MD: Author. (ERIC Document Reproduction No. ED444127)

Teal, W.H., & Shanahan, T. (2001). Ignoring the essential: Myths about fluency. *Illinois Reading Council Journal, 29*(3), 5–8.

Worthy, J., & Broaddus, K. (2002). Fluency beyond the primary grades: From group performance to silent, independent reading. *The Reading Teacher, 55*(4), 334–344.

Student Editions

Each Student Edition consists of twelve lessons and eight review pages. Each lesson begins with a four-page reading selection that is followed by four pages of comprehension, vocabulary, focus skill, and writing practice.

The reading selections include high-interest fiction and nonfiction written in a variety of literary genres, such as science articles, folktales, biographies, historical fiction, and others. Colorful photographs, inviting illustrations, and vibrant lesson openers support the text, aid in comprehension, and engage the reader.

The selections have visual supports appropriate to the content and skill, such as maps, timelines, charts, and diagrams. These visuals enhance the text and give students experience with a variety of informational formats.

Following each selection, students use a graphic organizer designed to teach the comprehension focus skill and provide a model for independent writing. Students then use the same or a similar graphic organizer to prewrite for an original story or article. The progression through the lesson helps students connect reading to writing.

Teacher's Guides

The Teacher's Guide includes a plan for each lesson. The easy-to-use lesson plans provide explicit reading comprehension and vocabulary instruction, as well as opportunities to extend the activities for individual needs.

Each lesson plan begins with a list of standards covered in the lesson for reading, vocabulary, writing, and, for nonfiction selections, the content area. Next, an oral language warm-up builds on background knowledge and is followed by an activity that introduces the vocabulary words.

Each lesson plan has a model Graphic Organizer transparency that teachers can use to introduce the comprehension focus skill and set the purpose for reading.

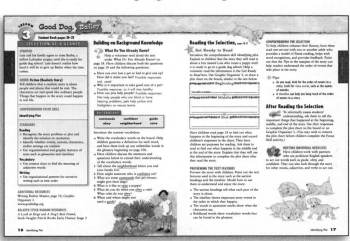

All lessons provide both formal and informal assessment opportunities. Each independent writing activity has a 4-point scoring rubric and a student writing rubric master to encourage student self-assessment.

Skills and Standards Chart

Title	Genre	Comprehension Focus Skill	Reading Standards	Vocabulary and Writing Standards	Content Standards
Lesson 1 *Meet Sue, the T. Rex Wonder!*	Nonfiction/Science Article	Identifying Main Idea/Supporting Details	• Identify main idea and supporting details in informational texts • Summarize information in texts, including central idea and supporting details • Use organizational and graphic features of texts such as glossaries and charts	**Vocabulary** • Use word context to find the meaning of unknown words **Writing** • Use organizational patterns for expository writing	**Science** Life Science: Organisms and environments
Lesson 2 *What a Long, Strange Trip!*	Fiction/Friendly Letters	Summarizing	• Summarize information in texts • Use organizational and graphic features of texts such as glossaries and photographs	**Vocabulary** • Use a variety of strategies to determine meaning and increase vocabulary **Writing** • Use graphic organizers to make a plan before writing a first draft	
Lesson 3 *Good Dog, Bailey*	Fiction/Realistic Story	Identifying Plot	• Recognize the story problem or plot and identify the solution or resolution • Identify whether events, actions, characters, and/or settings are realistic • Use organizational and graphic features of texts such as glossaries and timelines	**Vocabulary** • Use context clues to find the meaning of unknown words **Writing** • Use organizational patterns for narrative writing such as time order	
Lesson 4 *Don't Be Afraid of Bats*	Nonfiction/Persuasive Essay	Recognizing Author's Purpose	• Identify author's purpose • Recognize how language is used to persuade in informational texts	**Vocabulary** • Use sentence cues to construct meaning **Writing** • Write in different forms for different purposes such as to persuade	**Science** Life Science: Characteristics of organisms
Lesson 5 *Why Bears Sleep Through Winter: A Native American Legend*	Fiction/Legend	Making Predictions	• Make and explain inferences from texts such as making predictions • Understand basic characteristics of a variety of literary forms such as legends	**Vocabulary** • Use context clues to construct meaning and increase vocabulary **Writing** • Use organizational patterns for making predictions • State a prediction and an outcome based on clues	
Lesson 6 *Frogs and Toads*	Nonfiction/Science Article	Comparing and Contrasting	• Understand the use of comparison and contrast within a selection • Use organizational features of texts such as glossaries and diagrams	**Vocabulary** • Use word context to find the meaning of unknown words **Writing** • Use organizational patterns for expository writing such as compare and contrast	**Science** Life Science: Characteristics of organisms

Title	Genre	Comprehension Focus Skill	Reading Standards	Vocabulary and Writing Standards	Content Standards
Lesson 7 *Trouble on the Trail*	Fiction/ Humorous Story	Recognizing Setting	• Identify the importance of the setting to a story's meaning • Know basic characteristics of a variety of literary forms such as humorous fiction • Use organizational features of texts such as glossaries to locate information	**Vocabulary** • Use context clues to construct meaning and increase vocabulary **Writing** • Write brief narratives based on experiences, describing the setting in detail	
Lesson 8 *Amazing Animals*	Nonfiction/ Science Article	Identifying Fact and Opinion	• Distinguish fact from opinion • Identify author's purpose • Interpret and use graphs	**Vocabulary** • Use sentence context to identify the meaning of words **Writing** • Use organizational patterns for expository writing, such as fact and opinion	**Science** Life Science: Characteristics of organisms
Lesson 9 *Slue Foot Sue: The Best Catfish Rider of Them All*	Fiction/ Tall Tale	Understanding Realism and Fantasy	• Distinguish between reality and fantasy • Know basic characteristics of a variety of literary forms such as tall tales • Use organizational and graphic features of texts such as glossaries and illustrations	**Vocabulary** • Use context clues to construct meaning and increase vocabulary **Writing** • Write a brief, fantasy narrative	
Lesson 10 *Is the Loch Ness Monster Real?*	Nonfiction/ Social Studies Article	Identifying Cause and Effect	• Make and explain inferences from texts such as causes and effects • Understand factual information • Identify author's purpose	**Vocabulary** • Use word context to find the meaning of unknown words **Writing** • Use organizational patterns for expository writing such as cause-and-effect	**Social Studies** Time, Continuity, and Change: Demonstrate an understanding that different people may describe the same event or situation in diverse ways, citing reasons for the differences in views
Lesson 11 *The Mystery of the Missing Shell*	Fiction/ Mystery Play	Drawing Conclusions	• Make and explain inferences from texts such as drawing conclusions • Support conclusions with examples from text • Understand basic characteristics of literary forms such as plays and mysteries	**Vocabulary** • Use sentence context to find the meaning of unknown words **Writing** • Write a brief narrative based on the child's own experience	
Lesson 12 *Volcano: A Mountain of Fire*	Nonfiction/ Science Article	Sequencing	• Use specific information to relate sequences of events • Understand factual information • Use organizational and graphic features of texts such as glossaries and diagrams	**Vocabulary** • Use word context to find the meaning of unknown words **Writing** • Use organizational patterns for expository writing, such as time order	**Science** Earth and Space Science: Properties of Earth materials; Changes in Earth and sky

Colorful photographs and attractive illustrations create **engaging lesson openers** that support the fiction and nonfiction texts, aid in comprehension, and engage the reader.

LESSON 6

Frogs and Toads

What Do You Already Know?

Have you ever seen a frog or a toad? What did it look like? How did it move?

What Do You Already Know? taps into students' prior knowledge and develops oral language.

⭐ Get Ready to Read

An article can **compare** by telling how things are **alike**. It can **contrast** by telling how things are **different**. As you read, look for ways that frogs and toads are alike and different.

What is this animal leaping through the air? Is it a frog or a toad? It's hard to tell the two apart. They are alike in many ways.

Both the frog and the toad live in or near water. They both lay eggs in the water, too. The babies that grow from the eggs are called **tadpoles**. Tadpoles have tails that help them swim. Then they lose their tails. This happens as they grow into frogs or toads.

How They Look

A frog has smooth, sticky skin. It mostly lives in water. A frog's skin has to stay **moist**. A frog also has long back legs. Long legs help a frog leap far. The feet on a frog's back legs are **webbed**. The skin between a frog's toes helps it swim.

A toad is different. It has a short, fat body. A toad's skin is dry and bumpy. It spends more time on land than in water. A toad's feet are also webbed like a frog's. But a toad's legs are different because they are much shorter. Instead of leaping, a toad walks or hops.

VOCABULARY

tadpoles
(TAD pohlz) Young frogs or toads that live in water and have long tails but no legs

Tip
Words such as **alike** and **both** show that things are being **compared**.

VOCABULARY

moist (MOYST) Slightly wet

webbed (WEBD) Having skin between the toes

42 Comparing and Contrasting

Comparing and Contrasting 43

Get Ready to Read introduces the comprehension focus skill and helps students set a purpose for reading.

Subheads help students comprehend the structure of the text by "chunking."

Comprehension Tips support reading and help students apply the comprehension skill as they read. Key words "pop" in bold, red type.

Vocabulary words are highlighted in the text and defined, with pronunciation, at point of use. Each vocabulary word also appears in the Glossary.

VOCABULARY

poison
(POY zuhn) Something harmful to touch or taste

How They Stay Safe

The color of a toad helps it stay safe. A toad is brown and gray. It looks like the mud it lives in. An animal that wants to eat a toad may not be able to see it.

A toad also stays safe because it has a sack of **poison** behind each eye. When a toad is afraid, poison leaks out of the sack. Animals who eat the toad will get sick.

Like a toad, a frog uses its color to stay safe. However, most frogs are green and brown. They look like the water they live in.

A frog's eyes help it stay safe, too. The eyes **bulge** out on top of its head. A frog can see all around because its eyes stick out so far. When under water, the frog's eyes can still see above the water. The frog can look for **danger**. Then it can leap or swim away to safety.

Now that you know the difference between a frog and a toad, look back at that animal leaping through the air. Is it a frog or a toad?

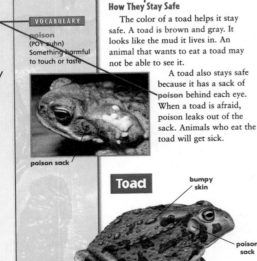

poison sack

Tip
Words such as **however** show that things are being **contrasted**.

VOCABULARY

bulge (BULJ) Stick out

danger
(DAYN juhr) Something that may cause harm

Toad
- bumpy skin
- poison sack
- short legs
- webbed feet

Frog
- bulging eyes
- smooth, sticky skin
- long legs
- webbed feet

44 Comparing and Contrasting

Comparing and Contrasting 45

Diagrams and other **visual supports** appear in each lesson to enhance the text and students' comprehension.

Comprehension Check provides opportunities to demonstrate comprehension of text on literal and higher, more inferential levels.

Comprehension Check

▶ Answer the questions below in complete sentences.

1. Where do frogs and toads lay eggs?

2. What happens to tadpoles as they grow?

3. What is this article mostly about?

4. What will a frog most likely do if it sees danger?

5. Why can a frog leap farther than a toad?

Vocabulary Builder

▶ Fill in the circle next to the best answer.

1. The word <u>danger</u> means—
   - Ⓐ something good
   - Ⓑ something that may cause harm
   - Ⓒ something short
   - Ⓓ something strong

2. The word <u>webbed</u> means—
   - Ⓔ having skin between the toes
   - Ⓕ having sticky skin
   - Ⓖ having gray skin
   - Ⓗ having smooth skin

3. The word <u>moist</u> means—
   - Ⓐ almost smooth
   - Ⓑ slightly wet
   - Ⓒ a little bumpy
   - Ⓓ very dry

4. The word <u>tadpoles</u> means—
   - Ⓔ the eggs of frogs and toads
   - Ⓕ water
   - Ⓖ young frogs or toads
   - Ⓗ bumpy skin

5. The word <u>poison</u> means—
   - Ⓐ something harmful to touch or taste
   - Ⓑ something happy
   - Ⓒ something safe
   - Ⓓ something that helps an animal hide

6. The word <u>bulge</u> means—
   - Ⓔ pull down
   - Ⓕ jump up
   - Ⓖ grow in
   - Ⓗ stick out

Vocabulary Builder provides strategies for confirming meaning and language development.
Test Preparation formats, which may also appear on the *Comprehension Check* page, equip students for success on standardized tests.

Your Turn to Write emphasizes major writing forms, purposes, and processes and connects reading to writing.

Focus Skill instructional box **reviews** the comprehension focus skill for each lesson.

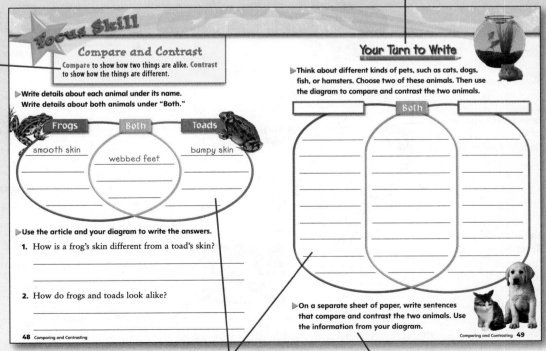

Focus Skill

Compare and Contrast
Compare to show how two things are alike. **Contrast** to show how the things are different.

▶ Write details about each animal under its name.
Write details about both animals under "Both."

Frogs — Both — Toads

smooth skin — webbed feet — bumpy skin

▶ Use the article and your diagram to write the answers.

1. How is a frog's skin different from a toad's skin?

2. How do frogs and toads look alike?

Your Turn to Write

▶ Think about different kinds of pets, such as cats, dogs, fish, or hamsters. Choose two of these animals. Then use the diagram to compare and contrast the two animals.

Both

▶ On a separate sheet of paper, write sentences that compare and contrast the two animals. Use the information from your diagram.

Graphic Organizers help students apply the comprehension focus skill and provide a model for independent writing.

A **Writing** prompt suggests ideas for independent writing in a variety of formats.

Clear **Standards** list benchmarks for reading, vocabulary, writing, and content areas.

Additional Resources are provided to enhance and extend each lesson.

Building on Background Knowledge taps into students' prior knowledge and provides questions that promote discussion.

Vocabulary provides ways to introduce each lesson's vocabulary words through engaging exercises.

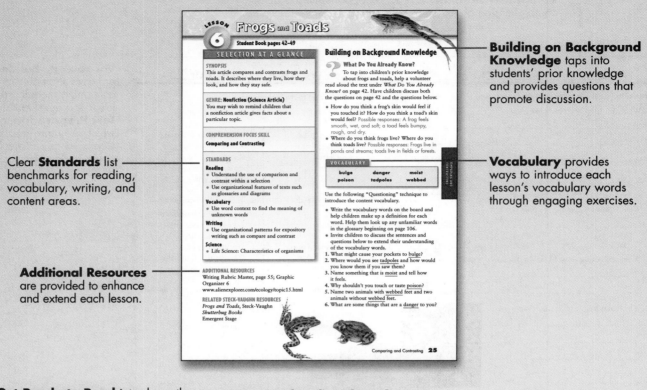

Get Ready to Read introduces the comprehension focus skill for each lesson, including a graphic organizer on a **Transparency** found at the back of this guide.

Comprehending the Selection checks comprehension, helps students improve fluency, and provides easy reference to the comprehension tips.

Reduced **Graphic Organizer** helps assess students' performance on the *Focus Skill* page.

Assessment aids teachers in checking students' comprehension after each reading selection.

Previewing the Text Features highlights the specific features and visual supports.

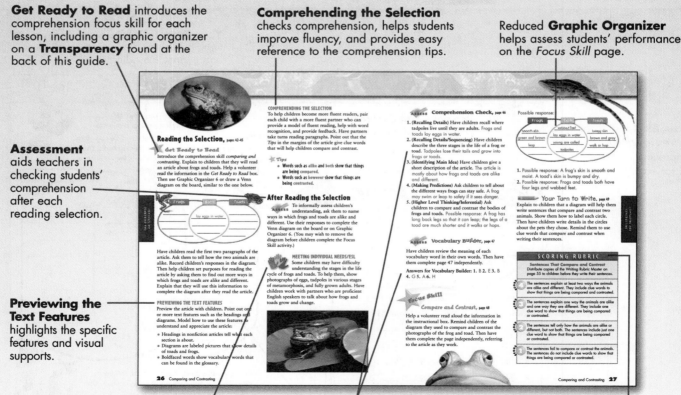

Meeting Individual Needs/ESL provides extended learning for different learner groups, including ESL students.

Answers and additional questions are provided for each activity in the Student Edition.

A 4-point **Scoring Rubric** provides teachers with a means to assess students' performance on each type of independent writing. For each lesson, a Writing Rubric Master for students based on this rubric is also provided.

Reading Skills	Level A	Level B	Level C	Level D	Level E	Level F
COMPREHENSION						
Literal Comprehension						
Understanding Facts and Details	•	•	•	•	•	•
Identifying Plot	•	•	•	•	•	•
Identifying Main Idea and Supporting Details	•	•	•	•	•	•
Summarizing		•	•	•	•	•
Identifying Text Structure						•
Interpretive Skills						
Retelling	•					
Distinguishing Fact from Opinion		•	•	•	•	•
Sequencing	•	•	•	•	•	•
Identifying Cause and Effect	•	•	•	•	•	•
Recognizing Setting	•	•	•	•	•	
Comparing and Contrasting	•	•	•	•	•	•
Critical Thinking						
Categorizing and Classifying	•	•				
Creative Response	•	•				
Understanding Realism and Fantasy	•	•				
Making Predictions	•	•	•	•	•	•
Drawing Conclusions		•	•	•	•	•
Identifying Author's Purpose		•	•	•	•	•
Analyzing Character			•	•	•	•
Making Inferences				•	•	•
Making Judgments					•	
Identifying Theme						•
VOCABULARY						
Naming Words	•	•				
Rhyming Words		•				
Classifying		•				
Context Clues	•	•	•	•	•	•
Synonyms	•	•	•	•	•	•
Antonyms			•	•	•	•
Words with Multiple Meanings			•	•	•	
Dictionary Skills			•	•	•	•
Prefixes			•	•	•	•
Suffixes			•	•	•	•
Compound Words			•	•	•	
Root Words			•	•	•	•
Analogies				•	•	•
Similes					•	•
Greek and Latin Roots					•	•

LESSON 1

Meet Sue, the T. REX WONDER!

Student Book pages 2–9

SELECTION AT A GLANCE

SYNOPSIS
This nonfiction article tells what scientists are learning from a *Tyrannosaurus rex* skeleton named Sue: that *T. rex* was most likely an excellent hunter that used its keen sense of smell to find prey.

GENRE: Nonfiction (Science Article)
Explain to children that a nonfiction article gives facts about a topic.

COMPREHENSION FOCUS SKILL
Identifying Main Idea and Supporting Details

STANDARDS

Reading
- Identify main ideas and supporting details in informational texts
- Summarize information in texts, including central idea and supporting details
- Use organizational and graphic features of texts such as glossaries and charts

Vocabulary
- Use word context to find the meaning of unknown words

Writing
- Use organizational patterns for expository writing

Science
- Life Science: Organisms and environments

ADDITIONAL RESOURCES
Writing Rubric Master, page 50; Graphic Organizer 1
www.kidsdomain.com/kids/links/Dinosaurs.html

RELATED STECK-VAUGHN RESOURCES
Dinosaur Fun Facts and *Dinosaur Show and Tell*, Steck-Vaughn *Pair-It Books* Emergent Stage 2

Building on Background Knowledge

What Do You Already Know?
Help a volunteer read aloud the text under *What Do You Already Know?* on page 2. Discuss with children the questions on page 2 and the questions below.

- How do we know what dinosaurs were like? Possible response: Scientists have shared what they have found by studying dinosaur bones and other fossils.
- What do you know about *T. rex*? Possible response: It was a big dinosaur.
- What can scientists tell by looking at the bones of animals that lived long ago? Possible responses: They can tell how big the animals were, how they moved, and what they ate.

VOCABULARY

brain	discovered	distance
fossils	skeleton	skull

Introduce the content vocabulary by building word knowledge as described below:

- Write the vocabulary words on the board. Help children make up a definition for each word, and help them look up any unfamiliar words in the glossary beginning on page 106.
- Read aloud the clues listed below. Have children provide a vocabulary word that fits each clue.

1. This is the part of your body that you use for thinking. brain
2. If you were the first person to find something, you could say you did this. discovered
3. These are parts of plants and animals from long ago that are found in rocks and the earth. fossils
4. This is a full set of bones from an animal or person. skeleton
5. If you measure how far away something is, you find this. distance
6. This protects your brain. skull

Reading the Selection, pages 2-5

Get Ready to Read

Introduce the comprehension skill *identifying main idea and supporting details*. Explain to children that they will read an article about what scientists know about a certain kind of dinosaur. Help a volunteer read the information in the *Get Ready to Read* box. Then use Graphic Organizer 1 or draw a main idea chart on the board, similar to the one below.

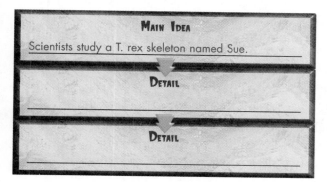

| **MAIN IDEA** |
| Scientists study a T. rex skeleton named Sue. |

| **DETAIL** |

| **DETAIL** |

Have children read pages 2 and 3 and then tell what they think the article is mostly about. Record their responses under the *Main Idea* section of the chart. Then have children set purposes for reading by asking them to look for details that tell more about the main idea. Explain that they will use these details to complete the chart later.

PREVIEWING THE TEXT FEATURES

Preview the article with children. Point out some useful text features such as the photographs, chart, and section headings. Model how to use these features to understand and appreciate the article:

- The photographs show some of the things that scientists found that helped them learn about dinosaurs.
- The chart gives basic facts about Sue in an easy-to-read format.
- The headings help show the main idea of each section of the article.
- Boldfaced words show vocabulary words that can be found in the glossary.

COMPREHENDING THE SELECTION

To help children improve reading fluency, have individuals read aloud with partners. Pair more fluent readers with less fluent readers to provide a model of fluent reading. Point out that the *Tips* in the margins of the article help children learn more about the article's main idea and details.

Tips
- Read the **heading** before each paragraph. It can tell you the main idea of that paragraph.
- Look for **details** in each clue. Think about how they connect to the main idea.
- Sometimes the main idea is shown in the **end** of an article.

After Reading the Selection

 ASSESS To informally assess children's understanding, ask them to tell what the article is mostly about. Then ask them to find some details that tell more about the main idea. Use their responses to complete the main idea chart on Graphic Organizer 1 or on the board. (You may wish to remove the chart before children complete the Focus Skill activity.)

MEETING INDIVIDUAL NEEDS/ESL

Have children work with partners to make picture dictionaries of key terms and concepts in the article such as *dinosaur, teeth, fossils, skeleton, skull,* and *brain*.

 Comprehension Check, page 6

1. **(Recalling Details)** Ask children how some animals can tell distance. Her eyes faced to the front.
2. **(Identifying Cause and Effect)** Ask children what they use their teeth for. To bite
3. **(Recalling Details)** Ask children what kind of food they must cut with a knife. Explain that Sue's teeth were like knives. Meat
4. **(Identifying Main Idea)** Explain that the title of an article should give clues to what the article is mostly about. Dinosaur Clues
5. **(Higher Level Thinking/Inferential)** Possible response: Scientists hardly ever find a dinosaur skeleton with most of its bones.

Vocabulary Builder, page 7

Have children tell the meaning of each vocabulary word in their own words. Then have them complete page 7 independently.

Answers for Vocabulary Builder: 1. distance **2.** skeleton **3.** skull **4.** brain **5.** discovered **6.** fossils

Focus Skill

Main Idea and Details, page 8
Help a volunteer read aloud the information in the instructional box. Recall with children the chart they used earlier to record the main idea and details. Then have them complete page 8 on their own, referring back to the article as needed.

Possible response:

MAIN IDEA
Sue's bones give clues about the past.

DETAIL
Sue's teeth were long and sharp.

DETAIL
The largest part of Sue's brain was for smelling.

1. Possible response: Dinosaur bones can give clues about the past.
2. Possible response: The skull showed that the eyes faced to the front.

Your Turn to Write, page 9
Explain to children that a main idea chart will help them write sentences about a dog or a cat. Tell children that they should include a main idea and two details when they write their sentences.

SCORING RUBRIC

Sentences About a Dog or a Cat
Distribute copies of the Writing Rubric Master on page 50 to children before they write.

4 The sentences tell about a dog or a cat. One sentence tells a main idea. Two more sentences give details that support the main idea.

3 The sentences tell about a dog or a cat. One sentence tells a main idea. One sentence gives a detail that supports the main idea.

2 One sentence tells a main idea or detail about a dog or a cat. Other sentences are missing.

1 The sentences are not about a dog or a cat, or there is not a complete idea about a dog or a cat.

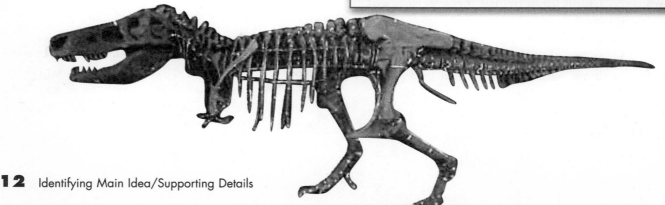

What a Long, Strange Trip!

SELECTION AT A GLANCE

SYNOPSIS
Through a series of letters to a friend, a girl describes her travels to some very unusual places, including a treehouse hotel, an ice hotel, and an underwater hotel.

GENRE: Fiction (Friendly Letters)
Explain to children that this story is told through a series of letters that a girl writes to a friend while she is on a trip. The places in the story are real, but the girl and her letters are not.

COMPREHENSION FOCUS SKILL
Summarizing

STANDARDS
Reading
- Summarize information in texts
- Use organizational and graphic features of texts such as glossaries and photographs

Vocabulary
- Use a variety of strategies to determine meaning and increase vocabulary

Writing
- Use graphic organizers to make a plan before writing a first draft

ADDITIONAL RESOURCES
Writing Rubric Master, page 51; Graphic Organizer 2
www.loggia.com/designarts/architecture/kids.html

RELATED STECK-VAUGHN RESOURCES
Homes Everywhere, Steck-Vaughn *Shutterbug* Emergent Stage

Building on Background Knowledge

? What Do You Already Know?
Help a volunteer read aloud the text under *What Do You Already Know?* on page 10. Have children talk about the question on page 10 and the questions below.

- Have you ever stayed in a hotel? What do you think you would see in most hotel rooms? Possible responses: beds, chairs, closets, bathrooms
- Look at the places in the photos. What do you think they would be like? Answers will vary.

VOCABULARY

bark	cases	rot
scrape	sway	thick

Introduce the content vocabulary.

- Write the vocabulary words on the board. Help children make up their own definition for each word, and help them look up any unfamiliar words in the glossary beginning on page 106.
- Read aloud the word pairs below. Have children identify the vocabulary word that belongs with each pair. Then discuss how all the words in each group are alike.
1. trunk, leaves bark
2. boxes, containers cases
3. swing, wiggle sway
4. spoil, die rot
5. rub, cut scrape
6. heavy, solid thick

Reading the Selection, pages 10–13

Get Ready to Read

Introduce the comprehension skill *summarizing*. Tell children that they will read a story about some unusual places that a family visited on a trip. Help a volunteer read the information in the *Get Ready to Read* box. Then use Graphic Organizer 2 or draw a summary web on the board, similar to the one below.

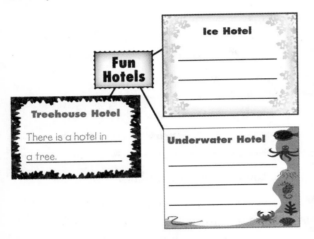

Remind children that a story may have more than one main idea. Each main idea should be included when writing a summary. Have children look at the photograph on the second page of the story and guess what the most important idea is on this page. Record their ideas in the *Treehouse Hotel* section of the web. Then have children set purposes for reading the selection by asking them to find other important ideas in the story. Explain that they will use these ideas to finish the web after they read the story.

PREVIEWING THE TEXT FEATURES

Preview the story with children. Point out some useful text features such as the photographs and the parts of the letters. Model how to use these features to enjoy the story:

- The photos show what the hotels look like.
- The greeting shows to whom the letters were sent. The signature shows who wrote them.
- Boldfaced words show vocabulary words that can be found in the glossary.

COMPREHENDING THE SELECTION

To promote children's fluency, have them read aloud with partners, taking turns reading alternating letters. Explain that the *Tips* in the margins of the selection help readers summarize.

⭐ Tips

- As you read, think about what each letter is **mostly** about. This will help you summarize the story.
- Use only the most **important ideas** in a summary.

After Reading the Selection

ASSESS To informally assess children's understanding, ask them to tell the most important idea of each letter and to summarize the entire story. Record their ideas on Graphic Organizer 2 or on the web on the board. (You may wish to remove the web before children complete the Focus Skill activity.)

MEETING INDIVIDUAL NEEDS/ESL

To develop concept vocabulary, have children point out and name objects in each photograph in the story. List the words they name on the board. Then encourage children to use each word on the list in a sentence.

ASSESS ## Comprehension Check, page 14

1. **(Sequencing)** Have children name the three places that Tyra visited in order. Tyra visited the underwater hotel last.
2. **(Identifying Cause and Effect)** Ask children if they have ever seen a rotten tree. Was it standing up straight? The tree and the treehouse could fall down.
3. **(Recalling Details)** Have children think of ways they could stay warm in a very cold place. Tyra wore a coat in the daytime. At night, she slept in a thick sleeping bag.
4. **(Drawing Conclusions)** Ask children what happens to ice in warm weather. Possible response: Cold weather keeps the hotel from melting.
5. **(Higher Level Thinking/Inferential)** Answers will vary.

ASSESS ## Vocabulary Builder, page 15

Have children review the meanings of the vocabulary words. Point out that this activity asks them to find words that rhyme with the vocabulary words. Then have them complete page 15 independently.

Answers for Vocabulary Builder: 1. lick **2.** lot **3.** may **4.** bases **5.** dark **6.** tape

 Focus Skill

Summarize, page 16

Help a volunteer read aloud the information in the instructional box. Remind children of the summary web they used earlier to record important ideas about the story. Then have children complete the page independently, referring to the story as needed.

Possible response:

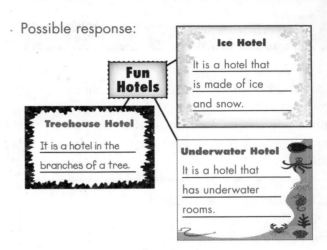

1. Possible response: Tyra stayed at three special hotels. One was made of ice, one was a treehouse, and one was an underwater hotel.

Your Turn to Write, page 17

Explain to children that a summary web will help them write a summary about a toy. Remind them to use information from the web when they write their summary.

SCORING RUBRIC

Summary About a Toy
Distribute copies of the Writing Rubric Master on page 51 to children before they write their summary.

4 The summary tells two important ideas about what the toy is like.

3 The summary tells what the toy is like, but may include details that are not very important.

2 The writing is about a toy, but is not a summary of what the toy is like.

1 The writing is not a summary. It does not tell about a toy.

Good Dog, Bailey

IDENTIFYING PLOT

SELECTION AT A GLANCE

SYNOPSIS
Luis and his family agree to raise Bailey, a yellow Labrador puppy, until she is ready for guide dog school. Luis doesn't realize how hard it will be to give up Bailey when the time comes.

GENRE: Fiction (Realistic Story)
Tell children that a realistic story is about people and places that could be real. The characters act and speak like ordinary people. Things that happen in the story could happen in real life.

COMPREHENSION FOCUS SKILL

Identifying Plot

STANDARDS

Reading
- Recognize the story problem or plot and identify the solution or resolution
- Identify whether events, actions, characters, and/or settings are realistic
- Use organizational and graphic features of texts such as glossaries and timelines

Vocabulary
- Use context clues to find the meaning of unknown words

Writing
- Use organizational patterns for narrative writing such as time order

ADDITIONAL RESOURCES
Writing Rubric Master, page 52; Graphic Organizer 3
www.guidedog.org

RELATED STECK-VAUGHN RESOURCES
A Look at Dogs and *A Dog's Best Friend*, Steck-Vaughn *Pair-It Books* Early Fluency Stage 3

Building on Background Knowledge

What Do You Already Know?
Help a volunteer read aloud the text under *What Do You Already Know?* on page 18. Have children discuss both the questions on page 18 and the following questions:

- Have you ever lost a pet or had to give one up? How did it make you feel? Possible responses: sad, upset
- Why is it important to take good care of a pet? Possible response: so it will stay healthy
- How can pets help people? Possible responses: Pets help people who are blind or have hearing problems; pets help police and firefighters on rescue teams.

VOCABULARY

commands	confident	guide
obey	neighborhood	raise

Introduce the content vocabulary.

- Write the vocabulary words on the board. Help children generate a definition for each word, and have them look up any unfamiliar words in the glossary beginning on page 106.
- Have children discuss the sentences and questions below to extend their understanding of the vocabulary words.
1. Tell about the <u>neighborhood</u> where you and your family live.
2. How might someone who is <u>confident</u> act?
3. What are some <u>commands</u> that pet owners might give their <u>dogs</u>?
4. What is it like to <u>raise</u> a puppy?
5. What do you do when you <u>obey</u> a rule? What rules do you <u>obey</u>?
6. When and where might you need a <u>guide</u>?

Reading the Selection, pages 18-21

Get Ready to Read

Introduce the comprehension skill *identifying plot*. Explain to children that the story they will read is about a boy named Luis who raises a puppy until it is ready to go to a guide dog school. Help a volunteer read the information in the *Get Ready to Read* box. Use Graphic Organizer 3, or draw a plot chart on the board, similar to the one below.

Beginning

Luis gets a puppy.

Middle

_____

_____

End

_____

_____

Have children read page 18 to find out what happens at the beginning of the story and record children's responses in the chart. Then have children set purposes for reading. Ask them to read to find out what happens in the middle and at the end of the story. Explain that they will use this information to complete the plot chart after they read the story.

PREVIEWING THE TEXT FEATURES

Preview the story with children. Point out the text features used in the story such as the section headings and the timeline. Model how to use them to understand and enjoy the story:

- The section headings tell what each part of the story is about.
- The timeline shows important story events in the order in which they happen.
- The words in quotation marks show what the characters say.
- Boldfaced words show vocabulary words that can be found in the glossary.

COMPREHENDING THE SELECTION

To help children enhance their fluency, have them read one-on-one with you or another adult who provides a model of fluent reading, helps with word recognition, and provides feedback. Point out that the *Tips* in the margins of the story can help readers understand the order of events that take place in the story.

Tips

- As you read, look for the order of events in a story. Look for **time words**, such as the names of months.
- A **timeline** can help you keep track of the order of events in a story.

After Reading the Selection

ASSESS To informally assess students' understanding, ask them to tell the important things that happened at the beginning, middle, and end of the story. Use their responses to complete the plot chart on the board or on Graphic Organizer 3. (You may wish to remove the plot chart before children complete the Focus Skill activity.)

MEETING INDIVIDUAL NEEDS/ESL

Have children work with partners who are proficient English speakers to act out words such as *guide, obey,* and *confident*. They can also look through the story for other nouns, adjectives, and verbs to act out.

Comprehension Check, page 22

1. **(Identifying Plot/Sequencing)** Ask children what might be a good title for the first part of the story. A
2. **(Comparing and Contrasting)** Ask children to tell how Bailey is like other puppies. Then ask if most puppies go to guide dog school. E
3. **(Sequencing)** Have children review the commands that Luis teaches Bailey and what Luis says each time Bailey obeys. B
4. **(Identifying Plot/Sequencing)** Have children discuss how the story ends. H
5. **(Higher Level Thinking/Inferential)** Possible response: It was hard for Luis to give up Bailey because she had become a part of his family.

 Vocabulary Builder, page 23

Have children tell the meaning of each vocabulary word in their own words. Then have them complete page 23 by asking a volunteer to read each sentence of the passage, pausing as children write the missing word.

Answers for Vocabulary Builder: 1. guide
2. raise **3.** neighborhood **4.** confident
5. commands **6.** obey

Plot, page 24

Help a volunteer read aloud the information in the instructional box. Recall with children how they used a plot chart earlier to record the important events from the story. Then ask children to complete the page independently, referring to the story as needed.

Possible response:

┌─────────── **Beginning** ───────────┐
│ Luis gets a puppy. │
└─────────────────────────────────────┘
             ▼
┌─────────── **Middle** ───────────┐
│ Luis teaches Bailey commands. │
│ Luis takes Bailey to many places. │
└─────────────────────────────────────┘
             ▼
┌─────────── **End** ───────────┐
│ Luis returns Bailey so she can go to guide dog school. │
└─────────────────────────────────────┘

1. Possible response: Luis takes care of Bailey, teaches her to obey commands, and takes her to busy places.
2. Possible response: This story is mostly about how a boy helps raise a dog that will be a guide dog one day.

 **Your Turn to Write,** page 25

Explain to children that a plot chart will help them write a story about a pet that they would like to have. Remind them to tell about the events in the order they happen as they write their story.

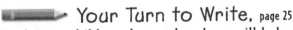

SCORING RUBRIC

Story About a Pet
Distribute copies of the Writing Rubric Master on page 52 to children before they write their story.

4 The story is about a pet. It has a clear beginning, middle, and end. The events in the story could happen in real life and are told in the order in which they happen.

3 The story is about a pet. The order of events is fairly clear and easy to follow. The events could happen in real life.

2 The story is about a pet, but the sentences do not show a clear beginning, middle, and end. The story includes some details that could not happen in real life.

1 The story is about a pet, but most of the events and details could not happen in real life. The events are also out of order and difficult to follow.

LESSON 4 DON'T BE AFRAID OF BATS

Student Book pages 26–33

SELECTION AT A GLANCE

SYNOPSIS
Many people are afraid of bats because they don't understand them. Bats are actually fascinating animals that are helpful to people.

GENRE: Nonfiction (Persuasive Essay)
Explain to children that authors write articles like this one to give their opinions about a topic and use facts to try to get the reader to agree with them.

COMPREHENSION FOCUS SKILL
Recognizing Author's Purpose

STANDARDS
Reading
- Identify author's purpose
- Recognize how language is used to persuade in informational texts

Vocabulary
- Use sentence context clues to construct meaning

Writing
- Write in different forms for different purposes such as to persuade

Science
- Life Science: Characteristics of organisms

ADDITIONAL RESOURCES
Writing Rubric Master, page 53; Graphic Organizer 4
dep.state.ct.us/burnatr/wildlife/kids/kpbats.htm

RELATED STECK-VAUGHN RESOURCES
Bats, Bats, Bats and *Bats at Bat*, Steck-Vaughn *Pair-It Books* Emergent Stage 1

Building on Background Knowledge

? What Do You Already Know?
Explore children's prior knowledge about bats by helping a volunteer read aloud the text under *What Do You Already Know?* on page 26. Have children discuss the questions on page 26 and the questions below.

- Why do you think some people are afraid of bats? Possible response: Some people think that bats get tangled in your hair and bite you.
- Do you think bats can be helpful animals? Why or why not? Possible response: Yes, they eat insects that could bite you.
- What would you do if you saw a bat? Answers will vary.

VOCABULARY

creatures	darts	echo
insects	mammals	pollen

Introduce the content vocabulary.

- Write the vocabulary words on the board and have children make up a definition for each word. Help them look up any unfamiliar words in the glossary beginning on page 106.
- Read aloud these riddles and clues and have children give a vocabulary word to answer each one.

1. We are a kind of animal that usually has hair or fur. Dogs and cats are part of this group. mammals
2. We are a kind of animal that has six legs and three body parts. Bees and ants are part of this group. insects
3. I am a yellow powder that can be found inside flowers. pollen
4. This is another name for animals. creatures
5. This is the way that something suddenly moves. darts
6. I am a sound that repeats itself. echo

Reading the Selection, pages 26-29

 Get Ready to Read

Introduce the comprehension skill *recognizing author's purpose.* Tell children that they will read an article about bats. Help a volunteer read the information in the *Get Ready to Read* box. Then use Graphic Organizer 4 or draw an author's purpose chart on the board, similar to the one below.

Author's Purpose

It is to tell people that bats are amazing creatures.

▼

Details

Bats help people.

_____

_____

_____

Explain to children that writers may have different reasons, or purposes, for writing, such as to tell a story, to share information, or to get readers to do or think something. Help children read page 26 and look for a detail that tells what the author thinks about bats: *They are amazing creatures that do things to help us.* Ask children what they think is the author's reason for writing the article. Record their ideas in the chart. Then have children set purposes for reading the article by having them find details that support this author's purpose. Explain that they will use these details to complete the chart after they read the article.

PREVIEWING THE TEXT FEATURES
Preview the article with children. Point out and model how to use some helpful text features such as the photographs and section headings:

- The photographs show what different bats really look like.
- The headings tell the main idea of each part of the article.
- Boldfaced words show vocabulary words that can be found in the glossary.

COMPREHENDING THE SELECTION
To promote children's fluency, have them read the article aloud with an adult helper. Have the adult read one paragraph at a time, pausing for the child to reread it aloud. Explain that the *Tips* in the margins of the article teach readers how to recognize the author's purpose.

 Tips

- As you read, ask yourself, "What is the author telling me? Why?"
- As you read, ask yourself, "What seems important to the author?"

After Reading the Selection

ASSESS To informally assess children's understanding, ask them to tell some details that helped them know that the author's purpose was to tell people not to be afraid of bats. Use their ideas to complete the author's purpose chart on the board or on Graphic Organizer 4. (You may wish to remove the chart before children complete the Focus Skill activity.)

MEETING INDIVIDUAL NEEDS/ESL
Have children draw a picture of something good that bats do. Then help them write a sentence about the picture. Have children share their picture and sentence with a small group.

Comprehension Check, page 30

1. **(Identifying Main Idea)** Have children tell in their own words what the article is mostly about. Possible response: Why Bats Are Helpful
2. **(Identifying Cause and Effect)** Have children recall some scary things they may have heard about bats. Possible responses: People believe things about bats that are not true; they don't know the good things that bats do.
3. **(Drawing Conclusions)** Discuss what the author's main message is. The author thinks bats are amazing creatures.
4. **(Identifying Main Idea and Details)** Have children quickly reread the section "Bats Help Us." Possible responses: Bats move pollen from plant to plant. Bats eat insects that are pests to people.
5. **(Higher Level Thinking/Inferential)** Possible responses: Some people harm bats because they don't know that bats are helpful. Other people build cities and roads where the bats used to live, destroying the bats' homes.

 Vocabulary Builder, page 31

Have children review the meanings of the vocabulary words. Then have them complete the page independently.

Answers for Vocabulary Builder: 1. C **2.** E **3.** D **4.** E **5.** C **6.** F

Author's Purpose, page 32
Help a volunteer read aloud the information in the instructional box. Remind children about the chart they used before they read the article to record details about the author's purpose. Then have them complete the page on their own, referring to the article as needed.

Possible response:

> **Author's Purpose**
> It is to tell people not to be afraid of bats.
>
> **Details**
> Bats help plants grow.
> Bats eat insects that are pests to people.

1. Answers will vary. Possible response: Yes, I learned that bats are good and don't hurt people. Now I'm not afraid of them.

➤ **Your Turn to Write,** page 33
Explain to children that using an author's purpose chart will help them write about an animal they think other people should like. Tell children to persuade readers to think the way they do by including facts that tell good things about the animal.

SCORING RUBRIC

Persuasive Sentences About an Animal
Distribute copies of the Writing Rubric Master on page 53 to children before they write their sentences.

SCORE 4 The sentences explain why people should like a certain animal. They include three or more details that support this purpose.

SCORE 3 The sentences explain why people should like a certain animal. They include two details that support this purpose.

SCORE 2 The sentences explain why people should like a certain animal. They include one detail that supports this purpose.

SCORE 1 The sentences are incomplete or are not about why people should like a certain animal. They do not include details to support the purpose of explaining why people should like a certain animal.

MAKING PREDICTIONS

SELECTION AT A GLANCE

SYNOPSIS
When Bear brags that he is the fastest animal in the forest, Turtle disagrees. The two decide to settle the matter by having a race. Bear loses and is so embarrassed that he returns to his cave and sleeps all winter.

GENRE: Fiction (Legend)
Tell children that some legends are old stories that tell why and how something in nature came to be the way it is.

COMPREHENSION FOCUS SKILL

Making Predictions

STANDARDS

Reading
- Make and explain inferences from texts such as making predictions
- Understand basic characteristics of a variety of literary forms such as legends

Vocabulary
- Use context clues to construct meaning and increase vocabulary

Writing
- Use organizational patterns for making predictions
- State a prediction and an outcome based on clues

ADDITIONAL RESOURCES
Writing Rubric Master, page 54; Graphic Organizer 5
www.angelfire.com/ma3/mythology/worldtalesindex.html

RELATED STECK-VAUGHN RESOURCES
Why the Leopard Has Spots and *How Spider Got Eight Legs*, Steck-Vaughn *Pair-It Books* Fluency Stage 4 and Early Fluency Stage 3

Building on Background Knowledge

What Do You Already Know?
Tell children that they will read about a bear and a turtle. The story explains why all bears now sleep through the winter. Then help a volunteer read aloud the text under *What Do You Already Know?* on page 34. Have children discuss the questions on page 34 and the questions below.

- Why do you think bears sleep during the winter? Answers will vary.
- What do you know about turtles? Possible responses: They have shells; they move slowly; many turtles live near water and can swim.

VOCABULARY

argue	brag	embarrassed
hibernate	punched	rapped

Introduce the content vocabulary.

- Write the vocabulary words on the board. Help children make up their own definition for each word, and help them look up any unfamiliar words in the glossary beginning on page 106.
- Use the following directives or questions to discuss the vocabulary words.
1. Tell about a time when you were <u>embarrassed</u>.
2. Name something you have <u>rapped</u> on.
3. Why might you <u>argue</u> with someone?
4. Name animals that <u>hibernate</u>.
5. If you were to <u>brag</u> about yourself, what would you say?
6. If someone took a hammer and <u>punched</u> the bottom of a can with a nail, what did the person do?

Reading the Selection, pages 34-37

Get Ready to Read

Introduce the comprehension skill *making predictions*. Explain to children that the Native American legend they will read is about a race between a bear and a turtle to see who is the fastest animal in the forest. Help a volunteer read the information in the *Get Ready to Read* box. Then use Graphic Organizer 5 or draw a prediction chart on the board, similar to the one below.

What I Think Will Happen

_____

▼

Clues That Helped Me

Bear looks like he's having trouble running.

_____

▼

What Happened

_____

Have children read the title and examine the illustrations to predict who will win the race. Also ask them to identify the clues that helped them make their predictions. Record their responses in the chart. Then have children set purposes for reading by asking them to read to find out what happens in the story. Explain that they will use this information to complete the prediction chart after they read the story.

PREVIEWING THE TEXT FEATURES

Preview the story with children. Point out the text features used in the story such as the illustrations and the quotation marks. Model how to use these features to understand and enjoy the story:

- The illustrations show what Bear and Turtle look like and what they do.
- The capitalized names of animals show that the animals act like people.
- The words in quotation marks show exactly what the characters say.
- Boldfaced words show vocabulary words that can be found in the glossary.

COMPREHENDING THE SELECTION

To help children become more fluent readers, you may wish to use the story as a readers' theater piece and have children take turns reading the parts for the different characters. Explain to children that the *Tips* in the margins of the story give readers information about making and checking predictions as they read.

Tips

- As you read, stop to think about the story. It will help you make a prediction about what will happen next.
- As you read, check to see if your last prediction was correct. How do you think the story will end?

After Reading the Selection

ASSESS To informally assess children's understanding, ask them to review the predictions they made before they read the story and the clues that helped them predict. Then have children tell if their predictions matched what happened in the story. Use their responses to complete the prediction chart on the board or on Graphic Organizer 5. (You may wish to remove the prediction chart before children complete the Focus Skill activity.)

MEETING INDIVIDUAL NEEDS/ESL

Write the words *brag, argue, punched, embarrassed, rapped,* and *hibernate* on the board and discuss their meanings. Then invite children to take turns pantomiming each word for the others in the group to guess.

Comprehension Check, page 38

1. **(Analyzing Character)** Ask children to recall what Bear says about himself before the race. proud
2. **(Drawing Conclusions)** Have children discuss how the other animals in the forest feel about Bear. They want Bear to stop bragging.
3. **(Drawing Conclusions)** Have children discuss the outcome of the race and how losing would make Bear feel. He is embarrassed and tired.
4. **(Sequencing)** Have children retell the events of the race. after the race is over
5. **(Higher Level Thinking/Inferential)** Possible response: Turtle thinks he is smart because he came up with a plan to win the race.

 Vocabulary Builder, page 39

Have children tell the meaning of each vocabulary word in their own words. Then help children complete the puzzle on page 39.

Answers for Vocabulary Builder:
Across: 3. rapped **6.** hibernate **Down:**
1. embarrassed **2.** argue **4.** punched **5.** brag

 **Focus Skill**

Predict, page 40

Help a volunteer read aloud the information in the instructional box. Recall with children how they used a chart to record predictions about the story. Then have them complete the page independently, rereading parts of the story as necessary.

Possible response:

What I Think Will Happen
Turtle will win the race.
Clues That Helped Me
Turtle talked to his brother and sister.
Turtle was in the lead.
What Happened
Turtle won the race.

1. Turtle had a brother or sister at each hole in the ice. Each time a turtle popped up, it made Bear think that Turtle was far ahead.
2. Bear had been beaten by an animal he thought was slower.

 Your Turn to Write, page 41

Explain to children that a prediction chart can help them predict what will happen in a story. After reading the clues on the chart, have children write what they think will happen and what actually happens in the chart. Then have children write sentences about what will happen next, including details about why the cat looks or acts as it does.

SCORING RUBRIC

Sentences About What Might Happen
Distribute copies of the Writing Rubric Master on page 54 to children before they write their sentences.

SCORE 4 The sentences tell what the cat does next or what happens to the cat as a result of its actions, based on information from the chart. The sentences give details about why the cat acts as it does. They are clearly written and easy to follow.

SCORE 3 The sentences tell what the cat does next or what happens to the cat as a result of its actions, but include only a few details about why the cat acts the way it does. The sentences are in an order that makes sense and are easy to follow.

SCORE 2 The sentences tell what happens to the cat, but what happens does not make sense. The sentences give few details about how the cat acts based on information from the chart.

SCORE 1 The sentences tell about the cat but do not tell what happens next. The sentences are poorly organized and hard to follow.

Frogs and Toads

Student Book pages 42–49

SELECTION AT A GLANCE

SYNOPSIS
This article compares and contrasts frogs and toads. It describes where they live, how they look, and how they stay safe.

GENRE: Nonfiction (Science Article)
You may wish to remind children that a nonfiction article gives facts about a particular topic.

COMPREHENSION FOCUS SKILL
Comparing and Contrasting

STANDARDS

Reading
- Understand the use of comparison and contrast within a selection
- Use organizational features of texts such as glossaries and diagrams

Vocabulary
- Use word context to find the meaning of unknown words

Writing
- Use organizational patterns for expository writing such as compare and contrast

Science
- Life Science: Characteristics of organisms

ADDITIONAL RESOURCES
Writing Rubric Master, page 55; Graphic Organizer 6
www.alienexplorer.com/ecology/topic15.html

RELATED STECK-VAUGHN RESOURCES
Frogs and Toads, Steck-Vaughn
Shutterbug Books
Emergent Stage

Building on Background Knowledge

❓ What Do You Already Know?
To tap into children's prior knowledge about frogs and toads, help a volunteer read aloud the text under *What Do You Already Know?* on page 42. Have children discuss both the questions on page 42 and the questions below.

- How do you think a frog's skin would feel if you touched it? How do you think a toad's skin would feel? Possible responses: A frog feels smooth, wet, and soft; a toad feels bumpy, rough, and dry.
- Where do you think frogs live? Where do you think toads live? Possible responses: Frogs live in ponds and streams; toads live in fields or forests.

VOCABULARY

bulge	danger	moist
poison	tadpoles	webbed

Use the following "Questioning" technique to introduce the content vocabulary.

- Write the vocabulary words on the board and help children make up a definition for each word. Help them look up any unfamiliar words in the glossary beginning on page 106.
- Invite children to discuss the sentences and questions below to extend their understanding of the vocabulary words.

1. What might cause your pockets to <u>bulge</u>?
2. Where would you see <u>tadpoles</u> and how would you know them if you saw them?
3. Name something that is <u>moist</u> and tell how it feels.
4. Why shouldn't you touch or taste <u>poison</u>?
5. Name two animals with <u>webbed</u> feet and two animals without <u>webbed</u> feet.
6. What are some things that are a <u>danger</u> to you?

COMPARING AND CONTRASTING

Reading the Selection, pages 42-45

⭐ Get Ready to Read

Introduce the comprehension skill *comparing and contrasting*. Explain to children that they will read an article about frogs and toads. Help a volunteer read the information in the *Get Ready to Read* box. Then use Graphic Organizer 6 or draw a Venn diagram on the board, similar to the one below.

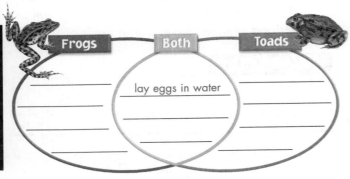

Frogs   Both   Toads

lay eggs in water

Have children read the first two paragraphs of the article. Ask them to tell how the two animals are alike. Record children's responses in the diagram. Then help children set purposes for reading the article by asking them to find out more ways in which frogs and toads are alike and different. Explain that they will use this information to complete the diagram after they read the article.

PREVIEWING THE TEXT FEATURES

Preview the article with children. Point out one or more text features such as the headings and diagrams. Model how to use these features to understand and appreciate the article:

- Headings in nonfiction articles tell what each section is about.
- Diagrams are labeled pictures that show details of toads and frogs.
- Boldfaced words show vocabulary words that can be found in the glossary.

COMPREHENDING THE SELECTION

To help children become more fluent readers, pair each child with a more fluent partner who can provide a model of fluent reading, help with word recognition, and provide feedback. Have partners take turns reading paragraphs. Point out that the *Tips* in the margins of the article give clue words that will help children compare and contrast.

⭐ Tips

- Words such as **alike** and **both** show that things are being **compared**.
- Words such as **however** show that things are being **contrasted**.

After Reading the Selection

ASSESS To informally assess children's understanding, ask them to name ways in which frogs and toads are alike and different. Use their responses to complete the Venn diagram on the board or on Graphic Organizer 6. (You may wish to remove the diagram before children complete the Focus Skill activity.)

MEETING INDIVIDUAL NEEDS/ESL

Some children may have difficulty understanding the stages in the life cycle of frogs and toads. To help them, show photographs of eggs, tadpoles in various stages of metamorphosis, and fully grown adults. Have children work with partners who are proficient English speakers to talk about how frogs and toads grow and change.

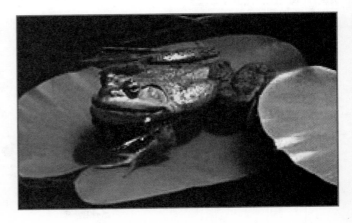

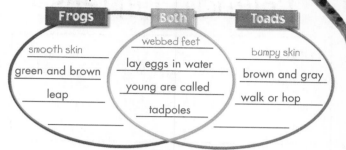

ASSESS Comprehension Check, page 46

1. **(Recalling Details)** Have children recall where tadpoles live until they are adults. Frogs and toads lay eggs in water.
2. **(Recalling Details/Sequencing)** Have children describe the three stages in the life of a frog or toad. Tadpoles lose their tails and grow into frogs or toads.
3. **(Identifying Main Idea)** Have children give a short description of the article. The article is mostly about how frogs and toads are alike and different.
4. **(Making Predictions)** Ask children to tell about the different ways frogs can stay safe. A frog may swim or leap to safety if it sees danger.
5. **(Higher Level Thinking/Inferential)** Ask children to compare and contrast the bodies of frogs and toads. Possible response: A frog has long back legs so that it can leap; the legs of a toad are much shorter and it walks or hops.

ASSESS Vocabulary Builder, page 47

Have children review the meaning of each vocabulary word in their own words. Then have them complete page 47 independently.

Answers for Vocabulary Builder: 1. B **2.** E **3.** B **4.** G **5.** A **6.** H

Focus Skill

Compare and Contrast, page 48

Help a volunteer read aloud the information in the instructional box. Remind children of the diagram they used to compare and contrast the photographs of the frog and toad. Then have them complete the page independently, referring to the article as they work.

Possible response:

Frogs	Both	Toads
smooth skin	webbed feet	bumpy skin
green and brown	lay eggs in water	brown and gray
leap	young are called	walk or hop
	tadpoles	

1. Possible response: A frog's skin is smooth and moist. A toad's skin is bumpy and dry.
2. Possible response: Frogs and toads both have four legs and webbed feet.

Your Turn to Write, page 49

Explain to children that a diagram will help them write sentences that compare and contrast two animals. Show them how to label each circle. Then have children write details in the circles about the pets they chose. Remind them to use clue words that compare and contrast when writing their sentences.

SCORING RUBRIC

Sentences That Compare and Contrast
Distribute copies of the Writing Rubric Master on page 55 to children before they write their sentences.

SCORE 4 The sentences explain at least two ways the animals are alike and different. They include clue words to show that things are being compared and contrasted.

SCORE 3 The sentences explain one way the animals are alike and one way they are different. They include one clue word to show that things are being compared or contrasted.

SCORE 2 The sentences tell only how the animals are alike or different, but not both. The sentences include just one clue word to show that things are being compared or contrasted.

SCORE 1 The sentences fail to compare or contrast the animals. The sentences do not include clue words to show that things are being compared or contrasted.

REVIEW

Student Book pages 50–51

Friendly Letters

SYNOPSIS
In this story, Leisha gets a letter from her best friend who is away at camp. Leisha makes a special card to let her friend know that she misses her.

GENRE: Fiction (Realistic Story)
Remind children that in a realistic story, the characters are made-up, but the events could happen in real life.

COMPREHENSION FOCUS SKILLS
Identifying Main Idea and Supporting Details
Comparing and Contrasting
Recognizing Author's Purpose
Identifying Plot
Making Predictions

Reviewing the Comprehension Skills

Review the following comprehension skills, which are presented in this story.

- **Identifying Main Idea and Supporting Details:** The main idea is what a story is about. The supporting details tell more about the main idea.
- **Comparing and Contrasting:** When you compare and contrast, you identify how two or more things are alike and different.
- **Recognizing Author's Purpose:** An author may write to give facts about a topic, to tell a story, or to get readers to think or do something.
- **Identifying Plot:** The plot is what happens to characters in the beginning, middle, and end of a story.
- **Making Predictions:** When you make a prediction, you tell what might happen next in a story. You can make predictions by using story clues and what you already know.

Reading the Selection, page 50

Get Ready to Read
Have children set purposes for reading. Invite them to read the title of the story and describe the illustration. Then have volunteers predict what they think the story is about. Children can then read to see whether the predictions were correct.

After Reading the Selection, page 51

ASSESS Comprehension Check

1. (**Identifying Main Idea and Supporting Details**) Have children tell in their own words what this story was mainly about. a girl who answers a letter
2. (**Comparing and Contrasting**) Have children name ways that Leisha's card and Jody's letter were alike and different. both had pictures
3. (**Recognizing Author's Purpose**) Remind children that authors may write to give facts, tell a story, or get someone to do or think something. tell a story about friends
4. (**Identifying Plot**) Have children tell why Leisha made the card for Jody. She was sad and lonely.
5. (**Identifying Plot**) Possible response: Leisha made a card to let Jody know that she missed her.
6. (**Making Predictions**) Possible response: Leisha will put the card in the mailbox.

MEETING INDIVIDUAL NEEDS/ESL
To reinforce children's ability to identify plot, have pairs of children work together to show what happens in this story. Have them circle the text that indicates the story's beginning, underline the text that indicates the middle, and draw a wavy line under the text at the end of the story. Then invite children to share their work and explain their reasoning.

Student Book pages 52-53

Fish and Whales

SYNOPSIS
This article tells how fish and whales are alike and different in how each animal gets the air it needs to breathe.

GENRE: Nonfiction (Science Article)
Remind children that nonfiction articles give factual information about a topic.

COMPREHENSION FOCUS SKILLS
Identifying Main Idea and Supporting Details

Making Predictions

Comparing and Contrasting

Recognizing Author's Purpose

Summarizing

Reviewing the Comprehension Skills

Review the following comprehension skills, which are presented in this article.

- **Identifying Main Idea and Supporting Details:** The main idea is what a story or article is about. The supporting details tell more about the main idea.
- **Making Predictions:** When you make a prediction, you tell what might happen next in a story. You can make predictions by using story clues and what you already know.
- **Comparing and Contrasting:** When you compare and contrast, you identify how two or more things are alike and different.
- **Recognizing Author's Purpose:** An author may write to give facts about a topic, to tell a story, or to get readers to think or do something.
- **Summarizing:** A summary gives the most important details and information from an article.

Reading the Selection, page 52

Get Ready to Read

Help children set purposes for reading. Then ask volunteers to read the title and describe the photos at the bottom of the page. Then have children predict what they will learn about in this article and read to see whether their predictions were correct.

After Reading the Selection, page 53

ASSESS Comprehension Check

1. **(Identifying Main Idea/Supporting Details)** Have children review what they know about a fish's gills. a flap of skin
2. **(Making Predictions)** Ask volunteers to recall how a whale breathes. take in air
3. **(Comparing and Contrasting)** Have children name some ways that fish and whales are alike. Then discuss how the animals are different. It has lungs.
4. **(Identifying Main Idea/Supporting Details)** Have children make up their own titles for this article. Remind them that a good title gives the reader an idea what an article might be about. How Fish and Whales Breathe
5. **(Recognizing Author's Purpose)** The author wrote this article to give information about how two different water animals breathe.
6. **(Summarizing)** This article explains that whales and fish both live in water, but have different ways of getting air. Fish have gills and whales have lungs.

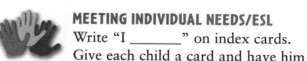

MEETING INDIVIDUAL NEEDS/ESL
Write "I _____" on index cards. Give each child a card and have him or her fill in the blank with one fact about whales or fish. (For example, "I have lungs.") Collect and shuffle all cards. Have each child pick a card, read the fact aloud, and tell whether the fact describes whales, fish, or both.

LESSON 7 Trouble on the Trail

Student Book pages 54–61

RECOGNIZING SETTING

SELECTION AT A GLANCE

SYNOPSIS

Two young girls accompany their father on a cattle drive in the 1800s. When the cattle refuse to cross a river, the girls help solve the problem.

GENRE: Fiction (Humorous Story)

Tell children that humorous fiction is like other fiction: it has characters, a setting, and a plot.

COMPREHENSION FOCUS SKILL

Recognizing Setting

STANDARDS

Reading

- Identify the importance of the setting to a story's meaning
- Know basic characteristics of a variety of literary forms such as humorous fiction
- Use organizational features of texts such as glossaries to locate information

Vocabulary

- Use context clues to construct meaning and increase vocabulary

Writing

- Write brief narratives based on experiences, describing the setting in detail

ADDITIONAL RESOURCES

Writing Rubric Master, page 56; Graphic Organizer 7
www.cowboyhalloffame.org

RELATED STECK-VAUGHN RESOURCES

My Prairie Summer and *Laura Ingalls Wilder: An Author's Story*, Steck-Vaughn *Pair-It Books* Fluency Stage 4

Building on Background Knowledge

What Do You Already Know?

Tap into children's prior knowledge by helping a volunteer read aloud the text under *What Do You Already Know?* on page 54. Have children discuss the questions on page 54 and the questions below.

- How do you think cowboys move cattle from one place to another? Possible response: Cowboys guide cattle with their horses.
- What would it be like to go on a cattle drive? Answers will vary.
- Where would you sleep and eat on a cattle drive? Possible response: You might eat outdoors and sleep on the ground.
- Would you like to go on a cattle drive? Why or why not? Answers will vary.

VOCABULARY

bandannas	boss	dusk
gear	herd	stampede

Introduce the content vocabulary.

- Write the vocabulary words on the board. Help children make up their own definition for each word, and help them look up any unfamiliar words in the glossary beginning on page 106.
- On the board create a word web with the word *cowboy* in the center. Ask children to think about how the vocabulary words are related to cowboys. Use their responses to create the word web. You may wish to keep the web for reference after children have read the story.

Reading the Selection, pages 54-57

Get Ready to Read

Introduce the comprehension skill *recognizing setting*. Tell children that they will read a story about girls on a cattle drive in the West about 150 years ago. Help a volunteer read the information in the *Get Ready to Read* box. Then use Graphic Organizer 7 or draw a setting chart on the board, similar to the one below.

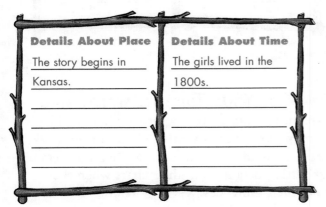

Details About Place	Details About Time
The story begins in Kansas.	The girls lived in the 1800s.

Explain to children that some stories take place in different times and places from the present. Explain that these details about time and place are called the *setting*. Have children read page 54 and look for details that tell about the time and place the story is set. Record their responses on the chart. Then have children set purposes for reading the story by asking them to find other details that identify the setting. Explain that they will use these details to complete the chart after they read the story.

PREVIEWING THE TEXT FEATURES

Preview the story with children. Point out some useful text features such as the illustrations and dialogue. Model how to use these features to enjoy and understand the story:

- The illustrations give readers a good idea of what the people and places look like, and what happens in the story.
- The words in quotation marks show exactly what the characters say.
- Boldfaced words show vocabulary words that can be found in the glossary.

COMPREHENDING THE SELECTION

To promote children's fluency, have them read aloud with a partner. Assign the more proficient partner to read the narrative section and the less fluent reader to read the dialogue. Explain that the *Tips* in the margins of the story give readers clues that help them understand the setting of the story.

Tips
- As you read, look for **place** names and **time** words.
- Look for **details** that help you picture the setting.

After Reading the Selection

ASSESS To informally assess children's understanding, ask them to identify details that tell about the place where the story happens and the time when it happens. Record their responses on the chart on the board or on Graphic Organizer 7. (You may wish to remove the chart before children complete the Focus Skill activity.)

MEETING INDIVIDUAL NEEDS/ESL

Tell children that they will go on a pretend cattle drive. Make name tags including *boss*, *cattle*, and *cowboy*. Have the "cowboys" tie bandannas over their faces. Then have children role-play tending a campfire, sleeping in bedrolls on the ground, and driving cattle on a trail and over a river. Encourage them to use words and ideas from the story as they role-play.

1. **(Identifying Main Idea)** Have children tell in their own words what the story is mostly about. girls on a cattle drive

2. **(Identifying Plot)** Ask children to tell what happened at the edge of the river and explain why this was a problem. The herd wouldn't cross the river.

3. **(Recalling Details)** Ask children what was unusual about the girls going on the cattle drive in the 1800s. Not many girls joined cattle drives.

4. **(Drawing Conclusions)** Ask children how they might act if they were proud of something they had done. they did a good job.

5. **(Higher Level Thinking/Inferential)** Possible response: They all went to sleep because it was dusk, and they had worked a long day.

 ASSESS **Vocabulary Builder,** page 59

Have children review the meanings of the vocabulary words. Display the web they began before reading the story and ask if they have any new ideas about how the vocabulary words are related to cowboys. Add their responses to the web. Then have children complete page 59 independently.

Answers for Vocabulary Builder: 1. gear **2.** stampede **3.** bandannas **4.** herd **5.** dusk **6.** boss

Focus Skill

Setting, page 60
Help a volunteer read aloud the information in the instructional box. Remind children about the setting chart they completed. Then have them finish the page on their own, referring to the story as needed.

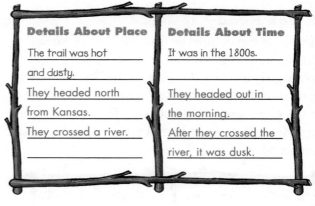

Possible response:

Details About Place	Details About Time
The trail was hot and dusty.	It was in the 1800s.
They headed north from Kansas.	They headed out in the morning.
They crossed a river.	After they crossed the river, it was dusk.

1. Answers will vary.

 **Your Turn to Write,** page 61
Explain to children that a setting chart will help them plan their own writing about a trail, park, or playground in the afternoon. Remind them to use setting details from their chart when they write their sentences.

SCORING RUBRIC

Sentences About a Place in the Afternoon
Distribute copies of the Writing Rubric Master on page 56 to children before they write their sentences.

SCORE 4 The sentences describe a trail, park, or playground in the afternoon. They include three or more details that describe the setting.

SCORE 3 The sentences describe a trail, park, or playground in the afternoon. They include two details that describe the setting.

SCORE 2 The sentences describe a trail, park, or playground but they may not be set in the afternoon. They include one detail that describes the setting.

SCORE 1 The writing is incomplete or not on the assigned topic. It does not include details describing the setting.

RECOGNIZING SETTING

AMAZING ANIMALS

Student Book pages 62–69

SELECTION AT A GLANCE

SYNOPSIS
There are many amazing animals in the world. This article tells about some of the world's fastest, smallest, and largest animals.

GENRE: Nonfiction (Science Article)
Remind children that a nonfiction article gives facts about a topic. It may also express the author's opinions.

COMPREHENSION FOCUS SKILL
Identifying Fact and Opinion

STANDARDS

Reading
- Distinguish fact from opinion
- Identify author's purpose
- Interpret and use graphs

Vocabulary
- Use sentence context to identify the meaning of words

Writing
- Use organizational patterns for expository writing, such as fact and opinion

Science
- Life Science: Characteristics of organisms

ADDITIONAL RESOURCES
Writing Rubric Master, page 57; Graphic Organizer 8
www.yahooligans.com/Science_and_Nature/Living _Things/Animals/

RELATED STECK-VAUGHN RESOURCES
Fantastic Animal Features and *The Amazing Animal Rescue Team*, Steck-Vaughn *Pair-It Books* Proficiency Stage 5

Building on Background Knowledge

? What Do You Already Know?
Invite children to share what they know about animals. Then help a volunteer read aloud the text under *What Do You Already Know?* on page 62. Have children discuss the questions on page 62 and the questions below.

- What animals do you think are amazing?
  Possible responses: shark, koala bear, elephant
- What do you think makes an animal amazing?
  Possible responses: its size, how fast or slow it moves, how long it lives

VOCABULARY

attack	common	interesting
prey	reptiles	tiny

Introduce the content vocabulary.

- Write the vocabulary words on the board and help children generate a definition for each word. Help them look up any unfamiliar words in the glossary beginning on page 106.
- Write *Amazing Animals* on the board. Help children make up sentences about animals and include the vocabulary words in the sentences. Write their sentences below the title and save them for later use.

IDENTIFYING FACT AND OPINION

Reading the Selection, pages 62-65

Get Ready to Read

Introduce the comprehension skill *identifying fact and opinion*. Explain to children that the article they will read includes both facts and opinions about animals. Help a volunteer read the information in the *Get Ready to Read* box. Use Graphic Organizer 8 or draw a fact-and-opinion chart on the board, similar to the one below.

FACTS	OPINIONS
The cheetah is the fastest land animal.	I think cheetahs are also the world's most beautiful animals.

Have children read the first paragraph on page 63 to find a sentence that is an opinion and a sentence that is a fact. Record their responses in the chart. Then help children set purposes for reading the article by asking them to find more facts and opinions as they read. Explain that they will use this information to complete the fact-and-opinion chart after reading the article.

PREVIEWING THE TEXT FEATURES

Preview the article with students. Point out one or more text features in the article such as the rulers that show the actual size of the world's smallest bird and fish. Then model how to use these features to understand and appreciate the article:

- Photos show the world's fastest, smallest, and largest animals.
- Rulers help readers see the actual size of animals.
- Boldfaced words show vocabulary words that can be found in the glossary.

COMPREHENDING THE SELECTION

To promote fluency, have children do choral readings of selected paragraphs about amazing animals. Point out that the *Tips* in the margins of the article will help children understand the difference between fact and opinion.

Tips
- Words such as "I think" or "I feel" show an opinion.
- Facts are true statements. As you read, ask yourself, "Can this be proven to be true?"

After Reading the Selection

ASSESS To informally assess children's understanding, have them identify facts and opinions in the article and tell how they figured out which was which. Use their responses to complete the fact-and-opinion chart on the board or on Graphic Organizer 8. (You may wish to remove the chart before children complete the Focus Skill activity.)

MEETING INDIVIDUAL NEEDS/ESL

Explain that the ending *-est* at the end of adjectives, or describing words, shows comparisons among more than two things. Have children identify these adjectives in the article. Write the words on the board. Then have children take turns asking and answering each other's questions such as *What is the fastest land animal in the world?* (The cheetah is the fastest land animal.)

IDENTIFYING FACT AND OPINION

ASSESS Comprehension Check, page 66

1. **(Comparing and Contrasting)** Ask children to recall the size of a bee hummingbird and what makes it different from all other birds. The bee hummingbird is about as long as a baseball card is wide.

2. **(Comparing and Contrasting)** Ask children to recall the size of the python and tell how it would look if it were in the classroom. The longest snake is as long as a school bus.

3. **(Drawing Conclusions)** Have children describe a Goliath spider. A Goliath spider eats insects and small reptiles.

4. **(Comparing and Contrasting)** Ask children to tell how the cheetah and sailfish are different from other animals. The cheetah can run about 65 miles per hour, and the sailfish can swim as fast as the cheetah can run.

5. **(Identifying Author's Purpose)** Have children recall the different reasons authors write: to entertain, to inform, or to persuade. The author probably wanted to inform readers about certain animals and to persuade readers that those animals are the most interesting.

 ## ASSESS Vocabulary Builder, page 67

Have children review the meanings of the vocabulary words and the sentences they created about the world's amazing animals. Then have children complete page 67 independently.

Answers for Vocabulary Builder: 1. prey
2. interesting **3.** tiny **4.** attack **5.** reptiles **6.** common

Fact and Opinion, page 68

Help a volunteer read aloud the information in the instructional box. Remind children of the chart they used earlier to note facts and opinions from the article. Then have them complete the page independently, reviewing parts of the article as needed.

Possible response:

FACTS	OPINIONS
The cheetah can run 65 miles per hour.	I think that cheetahs are beautiful animals.
The sailfish has a fin on its back.	I think it should have been called the "fastfish."

1. Possible response: The author feels that these animals are the most amazing in the world.
2. Possible response: The bee hummingbird is the smallest bird in the world.

 ## Your Turn to Write, page 69

Explain to children that using a fact-and-opinion chart can help them write their own sentences that give facts and opinions about an animal. Remind them to write complete sentences and include clue words that show opinions.

SCORING RUBRIC

Fact-and-Opinion Sentences
Distribute copies of the Writing Rubric Master on page 57 to children before they write their sentences.

SCORE 4 The sentences give at least two facts and two opinions about a familiar animal. The sentences are clearly written, well organized, and easy to follow. They include two or more clue words that signal opinions.

SCORE 3 The sentences give one or two facts and one or two opinions about a familiar animal. The sentences are organized and readable. At least one clue word is included to signal an opinion.

SCORE 2 The sentences focus on an animal that may or may not be familiar to the student. They state only one fact and one opinion, or may state only facts or opinions, but not both. It may include one clue word to signal an opinion.

SCORE 1 The sentences do not focus on just one animal and may state only opinions about several animals. The sentences are unclear, hard to follow, and incomplete.

SLUE FOOT SUE : The Best Catfish Rider of Them All

Student Book pages 70–77

SELECTION AT A GLANCE

SYNOPSIS

In this tall tale, Pecos Bill finally meets his match when he sees Slue Foot Sue riding a bucking catfish. They marry and raise a family. After their children are grown, Pecos Bill and Sue raise coyote pups as human children.

GENRE: Fiction (Tall Tale)

Tell children that tall tales are funny, made-up stories that have been told over and over again. The characters are often heroes, and many of the things that happen in the tales could never happen in real life.

COMPREHENSION FOCUS SKILL

Understanding Realism and Fantasy

STANDARDS

Reading
- Distinguish between reality and fantasy
- Know basic characteristics of a variety of literary forms such as tall tales
- Use organizational and graphic features of texts such as glossaries and illustrations

Vocabulary
- Use context clues to construct meaning and increase vocabulary

Writing
- Write a brief, fantasy narrative

ADDITIONAL RESOURCES

Writing Rubric Master, page 58; Graphic Organizer 9
www.pbskids.org/lions/pecos

RELATED STECK-VAUGHN RESOURCES

Carlita Ropes the Twister Steck-Vaughn *Pair-It Books* Early Fluency Stage 3

(side tab) UNDERSTANDING REALISM AND FANTASY

Building on Background Knowledge

? What Do You Already Know?

Help a volunteer read aloud the text under *What Do You Already Know?* on page 70. Have children talk about the question on page 70 and the questions below.

- Who are the main characters in some tall tales you know? What is special about these characters? Possible responses: Paul Bunyan and Babe the Blue Ox were giants and could do amazing things; John Henry could lay miles of railroad track very quickly.
- Could a person be raised by coyotes? Could a person ride a catfish? What kind of story might tell about someone who did these things? Possible responses: no; a tall tale
- Have you ever heard of Pecos Bill? What do you know about him? Answers will vary.

VOCABULARY

bucking	coyotes	lasso
mustang	ranches	rodeo

Introduce the content vocabulary.

- Write the vocabulary words on the board and help children generate their own definition for each word. Help them to look up any unfamiliar words in the glossary beginning on page 106.
- On the board write the first two words in each group below. Ask children to pick a vocabulary word that goes with each pair and explain the reasons for their selection.

kicking, jumping bucking
horse, pinto mustang
wolves, foxes coyotes
rope, loop lasso
farms, homes ranches
games, contest rodeo

Reading the Selection, pages 70-73

Get Ready to Read

Introduce the comprehension skill *understanding realism and fantasy*. Tell children that they will read a tall tale about a man and woman who did some very unusual things. Help a volunteer read the information in the *Get Ready to Read* box. Then use Graphic Organizer 9 or draw a realism/fantasy chart on the board, similar to the one below.

Could Really Happen	Could **Not** Really Happen
A man could see a catfish by a river.	A man could not be raised by coyotes.

Remind children that a tall tale may have some events that could really happen and some that could not really happen. Have children read page 70 and find one event of each kind. Write their responses on the chart in the appropriate sections. Then have children set purposes for reading by asking them to find other real and fantasy events as they read. Tell them that they will use these events to complete the chart after reading the tall tale.

PREVIEWING THE TEXT FEATURES

Preview the tall tale with children. Point out some useful text features such as the illustrations and dialogue. Model how to use these features to understand and appreciate the tall tale:

- The illustrations are funny and help readers imagine some of the events that could happen only in a fantasy.
- The words in quotation marks show what the characters say.
- Boldfaced words show vocabulary words that can be found in the glossary.

COMPREHENDING THE SELECTION

To promote reading fluency, have children read aloud with a partner, taking turns reading alternating paragraphs. Explain that the *Tips* in the margins of the tall tale explain more about telling the difference between a realistic story and a fantasy.

Tips

- As you read, ask yourself, "Could that **really** happen?"
- Think about what the characters **say** and **do**. Ask yourself, "Would a real person say or do this?"

After Reading the Selection

ASSESS To informally assess children's understanding, ask them to tell something from the tall tale that could happen and something that could not happen in real life. Record their ideas on Graphic Organizer 9 or on the chart on the board. (You may wish to remove the chart before children complete the Focus Skill activity.)

MEETING INDIVIDUAL NEEDS/ESL

Have children draw a picture of the part of the story they liked best. Ask them to share their pictures with a small group, explaining what they drew.

1. (Recognizing Setting) Ask children if they know in what part of the country most cowboys lived. B
2. (Comparing and Contrasting) Ask children to recall what kind of cowgirl Pecos Bill wanted to meet. F
3. (Drawing Conclusions) Ask children to describe what might happen if they push down on a spring. A
4. (Identifying Cause and Effect) Have children discuss what takes place at a rodeo. H
5. (Higher Level Thinking/Inferential) Answers will vary.

ASSESS **Vocabulary Builder,** page 75

Have children review the meanings of the vocabulary words. Then read aloud the passage on page 75. Reread each sentence, pausing as children write the missing word.

Answers for Vocabulary Builder: 1. ranches **2.** lasso **3.** mustang **4.** bucking **5.** coyotes **6.** rodeo

Focus Skill

Realism and Fantasy, page 76
Help a volunteer read aloud the skill information in the instructional box. Remind children about the realism/fantasy chart they completed. Ask them to tell other events from the story and tell whether they could really happen or not really happen. Then have children complete the page independently, referring to the story as needed.

Possible response:

Could Really Happen	Could Not Really Happen
A man could ride a horse.	A woman could not ride a catfish.
A man and a woman could get married.	A man and a woman could not raise coyotes as humans.

1. Possible response: This is a fantasy story. You can tell because the characters do things that could not happen in real life, such as riding a catfish and bouncing on a spring to the moon.

Your Turn to Write, page 77
Explain to children that a realism/fantasy chart will help them write their own fantasy story. Before they begin to write, remind them to use the ideas from their chart.

SCORING RUBRIC

Fantasy Story About Yourself
Distribute copies of the Writing Rubric Master on page 58 to children before they write their story.

4 The story is a fantasy about the child. It includes three or more details that could not happen in real life.

3 The story is a fantasy about the child. It includes two details that could not happen in real life.

2 The story is a fantasy that may or may not be about the child. It includes one detail that could not happen in real life.

1 The writing is incomplete or is not a fantasy story.

Is the Loch Ness Monster Real?

Student Book pages 78–85

SELECTION AT A GLANCE

SYNOPSIS
People have told stories about the Loch Ness Monster for about 1500 years, but is the monster real? The article tells why people do and do not believe in the monster.

GENRE: Nonfiction (Social Studies Article)
Remind children that a nonfiction article gives facts about a topic. It may also express the author's opinions.

COMPREHENSION FOCUS SKILL

Identifying Cause and Effect

STANDARDS

Reading
- Make and explain inferences from texts such as determining causes and effects
- Understand factual information
- Identify author's purpose

Vocabulary
- Use word context to find the meaning of unknown words

Writing
- Use organizational patterns for expository writing such as cause-and-effect

Social Studies
- Time, Continuity, and Change: Demonstrate an understanding that different people may describe the same event or situation in diverse ways, citing reasons for the differences in views

ADDITIONAL RESOURCES
Writing Rubric Master, page 59;
Graphic Organizer 10
www.nessie.co.uk

Building on Background Knowledge

What Do You Already Know?

Ask children to share what they know about strange creatures that supposedly exist around the world. Then help a volunteer read aloud the text under *What Do You Already Know?* on page 78. Have children discuss the questions on page 78 and the questions below.

- How do you decide if something is real or make-believe? Possible response: I look at the clues or facts.
- Why do you think people are so interested in the Loch Ness Monster? Possible responses: It is a big mystery that people want to solve; looking for a monster is exciting.

VOCABULARY

exist	fake	prove
reporters	shore	village

Introduce the content vocabulary by having children generate sentences as described below.

- List the vocabulary words on the board and help children make up a definition for each word. Record their definitions on the board. Help them look up any unfamiliar words in the glossary beginning on page 106.
- Tell children that the vocabulary words are from an article about the Loch Ness Monster. Have pairs of children use the words in sentences about the creature. For example:
1. People want to <u>prove</u> that Nessie really does <u>exist</u> and is not <u>fake</u>.
2. One person saw Nessie while walking along the <u>shore</u> near his <u>village</u>.
3. <u>Reporters</u> came to the <u>village</u> to talk to him.

- Record the sentences on the board and save them for use after children read the article.

IDENTIFYING CAUSE AND EFFECT

Reading the Selection, pages 78-81

⭐ Get Ready to Read

Introduce the comprehension skill *identifying cause and effect*. Tell children that they will read an article about the Loch Ness Monster. Help a volunteer read the information in the *Get Ready to Read* box. Then use Graphic Organizer 10 or draw a cause-and-effect chart on the board, similar to the one below.

Cause: Why It Happens	Effect: What Happens
People saw a photo of the monster.	People believed that the monster was real.

Have children study the photograph on page 80. Ask what effect this and other photos of the Loch Ness Monster likely had on people. Record their responses in the cause-and-effect chart. Then help children set purposes for reading by having them find other causes and effects related to the Loch Ness Monster. Explain that they will use this information to complete the chart after they read the article.

PREVIEWING THE TEXT FEATURES

Preview the article with children. Point out one or more text features such as the photographs and captions. Model how to use these features to get the most out of the article:

- The photos show what the "monster" and Loch Ness, Scotland, look like.
- The captions tell readers what they need to know about the photos.
- Boldfaced words show vocabulary words that can be found in the glossary.

COMPREHENDING THE SELECTION

To help children become more fluent, have them read aloud simultaneously or echo read with an audiotaped reading of the article. Point out to children that the *Tips* in the margins of the article will help them identify causes and effects.

⭐ Tips

- Words such as **because** tell you about cause and effect.
- As you read, look for clue words such as **so** and **caused** to find out why things happened.

After Reading the Selection

ASSESS To informally assess children's understanding, have them tell the causes of opinions discussed in the article. Use their ideas to fill in the cause-and-effect chart on the board or on Graphic Organizer 10. (You may wish to remove the chart before children complete the Focus Skill activity.)

MEETING INDIVIDUAL NEEDS/ESL

To help children comprehend what Loch Ness is and where it is located, display a map of Scotland and point out some of its features. Remind children that a lake, or *loch* in Scottish, is a body of water surrounded by land. Help children locate Loch Ness on the map and display additional photographs to show its size. Then encourage children to make up sentences about the lake, Scotland, and the Loch Ness Monster.

IDENTIFYING CAUSE AND EFFECT

Comprehension Check, page 82

1. **(Recalling Details)** Remind children that *loch* is a Scottish word that means lake. Then have children reread the first and last paragraphs of the article. Loch Ness is in Scotland.

2. **(Recognizing Author's Purpose)** Have children recall some reasons authors have for writing: to entertain, to inform, or to persuade. The author wanted to inform readers about the Loch Ness Monster and why some people believe it exists and why others do not.

3. **(Recalling Details)** Have children tell what some people think might be in Loch Ness. Possible response: A dinosaur or a giant otter might be in the lake.

4. **(Identifying Fact and Opinion)** Remind children that an opinion is what one person thinks and a fact is something that can be proven. Possible response: Nessie is one of the world's greatest mysteries.

5. **(Higher Level Thinking/Inferential)** Possible response: People have been talking about Nessie for about 1500 years, so people will probably keep trying to spot her.

 Vocabulary Builder, page 83

Have children recall the meaning of each vocabulary word and review the sentences they generated. Then have them complete page 83 independently.

Answers for Vocabulary Builder: 1. land by the water **2.** a small town **3.** people who tell the news **4.** to show that something is a fact **5.** to live or be real **6.** not real

Cause and Effect, page 84
Help a volunteer read aloud the information in the instructional box. Remind children of the chart they used earlier. Then have them complete the page independently, referring to the article as needed.

Cause: Why It Happens	Effect: What Happens
People say they have seen the Loch Ness Monster. _____	Some people _____ believe _____ in the Loch Ness Monster.
Scientists cannot prove there is a monster. _____	Some people _____ do not believe _____ in the Loch Ness Monster.

1. Answers will vary.

 Your Turn to Write, page 85
Tell children that a cause-and-effect chart will help them write their own sentences about a time they did well in a school activity or playing a sport. Remind them to include causes and effects in their sentences.

SCORING RUBRIC

Cause-and-Effect Sentences
Distribute copies of the Writing Rubric Master on page 59 to children before they write their sentences.

4 The sentences are about a time the child did well in a school activity or playing a sport. They include one or two causes that tell why the child did well and one or two effects that tell what happened. The sentences are well-written, in an order that makes sense, and easy to read.

3 The sentences are about a time the child did well in an activity or sport, but include only one cause that tells why the child did well and one effect that tells what happened. The sentences are clear and organized.

2 The sentences tell one effect about a time the child did well in a school activity or playing a sport, but do not describe the cause that brought about the effect. The sentences are readable.

1 The sentences may not be about a time the child did well in a school activity or playing a sport. They are missing both causes and effects.

IDENTIFYING CAUSE AND EFFECT

The Mystery of the Missing Shell

Student Book pages 86–93

SELECTION AT A GLANCE

SYNOPSIS
Will and Beth finish their sand castle and top it with the perfect shell. Moments later the shell disappears. Beth's dad and the children put some clues together to solve the mystery of the missing shell.

GENRE: Fiction (Mystery Play)
Explain to children that a play is a story written for actors on the stage, in a movie, or on television. A mystery is a story in which the characters use clues to solve something puzzling.

COMPREHENSION FOCUS SKILL
Drawing Conclusions

STANDARDS
Reading
- Make and explain inferences from texts such as drawing conclusions
- Support conclusions with examples from text
- Understand basic characteristics of literary forms such as plays and mysteries

Vocabulary
- Use sentence context to find the meaning of unknown words

Writing
- Write a brief narrative based on the child's own experience

ADDITIONAL RESOURCES
Writing Rubric Master, page 60; Graphic Organizer 11
www.childrenstheatreplays.com

RELATED STECK-VAUGHN RESOURCES
The Mystery of the Missing Leopard, Steck-Vaughn *Pair-It Books* Proficiency Stage 5

Building on Background Knowledge

What Do You Already Know?
Tap into children's prior knowledge about mysteries. Help a volunteer read aloud the text that is under *What Do You Already Know?* on page 86. Discuss the questions on page 86 and the questions below.

- What kinds of things happen in some mysteries you know about? Answers will vary.
- What do the main characters in a mystery try to do? How do they do it? Possible responses: The main characters try to solve the mystery or problem. The main characters look for clues and put them together in a way that solves the mystery.
- What kinds of clues might a character in a mystery look for to find something that is missing? Answers will vary.

VOCABULARY

decorate	foundation	moat
perfect	surf	tide

Introduce the content vocabulary.

- List the vocabulary words on the board, and help children generate a definition for each one. Help them look up any unfamiliar words in the glossary beginning on page 106.
- Tell children that the words are from a play in which two children build a sand castle at the beach. Have children work in pairs or small groups to use the vocabulary words in sentences about building a sand castle at the beach. For example:
1. Pack down the sand to make a <u>perfect</u> <u>foundation</u> for your sand castle.
2. If you get too close to the <u>surf</u>, your sand castle will wash away when the <u>tide</u> comes in.
3. You can <u>decorate</u> your sand castle with seaweed and shells and dig a <u>moat</u> around the <u>foundation</u>.

- Record the sentences and save them for use after children have read the play.

DRAWING CONCLUSIONS

Reading the Selection, pages 86-89

⭐ Get Ready to Read

Introduce the comprehension skill *drawing conclusions*. Explain to children that they will read a play in which two children solve a mystery. Help a volunteer read the information in the *Get Ready to Read* box. Then use Graphic Organizer 11 or draw a conclusion chart on the board, similar to the one below.

Problem
The shell is missing from the sand castle.

▽

Clues
Beth's dad sees animal tracks.

▽

My Conclusion

Have children skim pages 86 and 87 of the play twice—first, to find out what mystery the children have to solve, and second, to identify clues that may help them solve the mystery. Record their responses in the chart. Then help children set purposes for reading the play by asking them to find more clues that can help solve the mystery of the missing seashell. Explain that they will use this information to complete the chart after reading the play.

PREVIEWING THE TEXT FEATURES

Preview the play with children. Point out one or more text features in the play, such as how to tell who is speaking. Model how to use these features to understand and enjoy the play:

- The characters' names are listed along the left side of the page. This shows the exact words that the characters say.
- The illustrations show what the characters and setting look like.
- Boldfaced words show vocabulary words that can be found in the glossary.

COMPREHENDING THE SELECTION

To help children become more fluent readers, have groups of three read the story aloud as a reader's theater piece, with children taking turns reading aloud the characters' dialogue. Point out that the *Tips* in the margins of the play will help children draw conclusions to solve the mystery of the missing shell.

⭐ Tips

- If you saw some tracks around the sand castle, what **conclusion** might you draw?
- When you read a story, stop to think about different **conclusions** that **make sense**.

After Reading the Selection

 To informally assess children's understanding, ask them to tell what conclusions they or the characters drew from the clues in the play to solve the mystery of the missing shell. Use their responses to complete the conclusion chart on the board or on Graphic Organizer 11. (You may wish to remove the chart before children complete the Focus Skill activity.)

MEETING INDIVIDUAL NEEDS/ESL

For children who may be unfamiliar with hermit crabs and their behavior, provide them with basic information and photos. Explain that a hermit crab has soft body parts. It protects its soft parts by climbing into an empty shell. When the hermit crab grows too big for the shell, it finds a bigger one. The crab's claws are usually outside the shell unless the hermit crab pulls them inside. That is why Will and Beth probably didn't realize the shells they used to decorate the sand castle were hermit crab homes. Ask children to describe the hermit crabs they see in the illustrations and tell what is happening in the play.

Possible response:

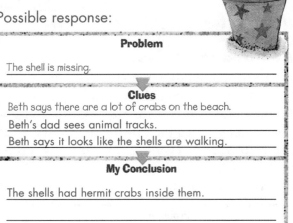

1. **(Identifying Setting)** Have children look at the illustrations to understand where the play takes place. B
2. **(Sequencing)** Have children look at the illustrations on pages 86 and 87 and tell what happens. H
3. **(Drawing Conclusions)** Have children think about a time when something disappeared and how they felt about it. A
4. **(Drawing Conclusions)** Have children review the text at the beginning of the play and discuss what Will and Beth say about building sand castles. F
5. **(Higher Level Thinking/Inferential)** Possible response: This story could really happen because hermit crabs are real and live in shells.

Problem

The shell is missing.

Clues

Beth says there are a lot of crabs on the beach.

Beth's dad sees animal tracks.

Beth says it looks like the shells are walking.

My Conclusion

The shells had hermit crabs inside them.

1. Possible response: Will says the shells they put on the sand castle must have had hermit crabs inside them.

✓ ASSESS **Vocabulary Builder,** page 91

Have children review the sentences they generated before reading the play and then tell the meaning of each vocabulary word in their own words. Then have them complete page 91 independently.

Answers for Vocabulary Builder: 1. tide
2. foundation **3.** moat **4.** decorate
5. perfect **6.** surf

Focus Skill

Draw Conclusions, page 92
Help a volunteer read aloud the information in the instructional box. Remind children of the chart they used earlier to record the mystery and some clues that could help solve the mystery. Then have them complete the page on their own, rereading parts of the play as needed.

Your Turn to Write, page 93
Tell children that a conclusion chart will help them write sentences about a time when they lost something and then found it. Before they write, remind them to include clues and what they knew that helped them find the missing object.

SCORING RUBRIC

Mystery Sentences
Distribute copies of the Writing Rubric Master on page 60 to children before they write their sentences.

4 The sentences tell about something lost and found and include three or more clues the child used, the conclusion, and the final outcome.

3 The sentences tell about something lost and found. They include only one or two clues and the child's conclusion, but may or may not tell the final outcome.

2 The sentences may simply tell about something that was lost and found, but do not include any clues or the child's conclusion.

1 The sentences tell that something was missing or that something was found, but not both. There are no clues or a conclusion.

DRAWING CONCLUSIONS

Volcano: A Mountain of Fire

Student Book pages 94–101

SELECTION AT A GLANCE

SYNOPSIS
This nonfiction article gives a step-by-step explanation of how a volcano erupts.

GENRE: Nonfiction (Science Article)
Tell children that a nonfiction article gives facts about real things or events. Some articles explain how things happen.

COMPREHENSION FOCUS SKILL
Sequencing

STANDARDS
Reading
- Use specific information to relate sequences of events
- Understand factual information
- Use organizational and graphic features of texts such as glossaries and diagrams

Vocabulary
- Use word context to find the meaning of unknown words

Writing
- Use organizational patterns for expository writing, such as time order

Science
- Earth and Space Science: Properties of Earth materials; Changes in Earth

ADDITIONAL RESOURCES
Writing Rubric Master, page 61; Graphic Organizer 12
www.fema/kids/volfacts.htm

RELATED STECK-VAUGHN RESOURCES
Volcanos, Steck-Vaughn *What About...?* Books

Building on Background Knowledge

? What Do You Already Know?
Help a volunteer read aloud the text under *What Do You Already Know?* on page 94. Have children talk about the questions on page 94 and the questions below.

- Have you ever seen pictures of volcanoes? What do they look like? Possible response: They look like mountains with smoke, fire, and melted rock flowing from them.
- What do you think makes volcanoes erupt or explode? Answers will vary.

VOCABULARY

erupts	flows	forces
liquid	swell	trapped

Introduce the content vocabulary.

- Write the vocabulary words on the board. Help children make up their own definition for each word, and help them look up any unfamiliar words in the glossary beginning on page 106.
- Tell children to imagine that you are filling a big balloon with water. Ask what would happen if you squeezed the water-filled balloon. Help them use the vocabulary words to describe what might happen to the water and the balloon.
1. Water is <u>trapped</u> inside the balloon.
2. It <u>forces</u> the balloon to <u>swell</u>.
3. The <u>liquid</u> <u>erupts</u> from the opening.
4. It <u>flows</u> all over the floor.

- Write children's sentences on the board. Keep them for later use.

Reading the Selection, pages 94-97

⭐ Get Ready to Read

Introduce the comprehension skill *sequencing.*
Tell children that they will read an article about
how volcanoes erupt. Help a volunteer read the
information in the *Get Ready to Read* box. Then
use Graphic Organizer 12 or draw a sequencing
chart on the board, similar to the one below.

First, the magma forms a pool.

↓

Next, _____

_____

↓

Then, _____

_____

↓

Last, _____

_____

Remind children that an article can explain how
something happens. It may tell about different
steps or events in the order they happen. Have
children look at the section heading on page 95
and tell what happens first inside a volcano.
Record their responses in the *First* box of the
sequence chart. Then have children set purposes
for reading the article by asking them to find out
what other things happen in a volcano. Tell them
that they will use this information to finish the
chart after they read the article.

PREVIEWING THE TEXT FEATURES

Preview the article with children. Point out some
important text features, including the photographs,
diagram, captions, and section headings. Model
how to use these features to understand and enjoy
the article:

- The photos show what a volcano looks like.
- The captions explain what is shown in the
photos.

- The diagram explains what happens inside the
volcano.
- The headings tell what each section is about.
- Boldfaced words show vocabulary words that
can be found in the glossary.

COMPREHENDING THE SELECTION

To promote children's fluency, have them whisper-
read along with an adult helper or another fluent
reader. Explain that the *Tips* in the margins of the
article give clue words that tell the sequence, or
order, of events.

⭐ Tips

- Words such as **first** give clues that something
happens in an order.
- Clue words such as **next**, **then**, and **last** show
sequence.

After Reading the Selection

ASSESS To informally assess children's
understanding, ask them to tell the
most important events that take place inside a
volcano before it erupts. Record their responses
on Graphic Organizer 12 or on the board. (You
may wish to remove the chart before children
complete the Focus Skill activity.)

MEETING INDIVIDUAL NEEDS/ESL

To develop concept knowledge and
expand vocabulary, have children
role-play the different events inside the volcano.
First, show pictures as you talk about the process.
Then have some children take the roles of magma
and gas while others form the wall of the volcano.
You may wish to prepare colored nametags that
name each role. Encourage children to act out and
then retell the process in their own words.

ASSESS Comprehension Check, page 98

1. **(Identifying Main Idea)** Explain that the title of the article can give clues to what the article is mostly about. The article is mostly about what happens when a volcano erupts.
2. **(Recalling Details)** Have children look at the first paragraph in the article to find the answer. Magma is liquid rock.
3. **(Recalling Details)** Have children describe the temperature inside the earth. Magma is rock that melts inside the earth.
4. **(Drawing Conclusions)** Ask children what might happen to a tree that was in a fire. Possible response: The tree could get covered with ash or it could burn up.
5. **(Higher Level Thinking/Inferential)** A volcano becomes a mountain of fire when burning lava erupts from it.

 ASSESS Vocabulary Builder, page 99

Have children review the meanings of the vocabulary words. Review the sentences they generated before reading the article. Then have them complete page 99 independently.

Answers for Vocabulary Builder: 1. grow **2.** stuck **3.** moves **4.** like water **5.** pushes **6.** bursts

 Focus Skill

Sequence, page 100

Help a volunteer read aloud the skill information in the instructional box. Recall with children the sequence chart they began earlier that tells about the events that take place before a volcano erupts. Then have them complete the page on their own.

Possible response:

First, the magma forms a pool.
Next, the magma fills the volcano.
Then, magma forms a hard cover.
Last, the volcano erupts.

1. Possible response: As magma flows from the volcano, it becomes burning lava.

 Your Turn to Write, page 101

Explain to children that a sequence chart will help them write their own sentences about something they know how to do. Have children write three or four sentences using information from their chart to show the steps describing something they know how to do. Remind them to use clue words to describe the order of the steps.

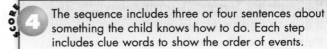

SCORING RUBRIC

Write About How To Do Something
Distribute copies of the Writing Rubric Master on page 61 to children before they write.

SCORE 4 The sequence includes three or four sentences about something the child knows how to do. Each step includes clue words to show the order of events.

SCORE 3 The sequence includes three sentences about something the child knows how to do. Some steps use clue words to show the order of events.

SCORE 2 The sequence includes two sentences about something the child knows how to do. One sentence may include a clue word to show the order of events.

SCORE 1 The sequence is not complete or is not an explanation of something the child knows how to do.

REVIEW

Why Bats Fly at Night
A Folktale

SYNOPSIS

Eagle demands that Bat pay "flying money" as other birds must do. Bat insists that he is not a bird, but finally escapes by hiding in a cave. This explains why bats live in caves and only fly at night.

GENRE: Fiction (Folktale)

Explain to children that a folktale is a made-up story that explains why something is the way it is.

COMPREHENSION FOCUS SKILLS

Recognizing Setting

Drawing Conclusions

Sequencing

Understanding Realism and Fantasy

Reviewing the Comprehension Skills

Review the following comprehension skills, which are presented in this folktale.

- **Recognizing Setting:** A setting is where and when a story takes place.
- **Drawing Conclusions:** Authors do not always tell you everything. Sometimes you must use clues from the story, along with what you already know, to draw conclusions.
- **Sequencing:** The sequence is the order in which events happen.
- **Understanding Realism and Fantasy:** A realistic story tells about things that could happen in real life. A fantasy story tells about things that could not really happen.

Reading the Selection, page 102

 Get Ready to Read

Help children set purposes for reading. Then ask volunteers to read the title and describe the illustration. Then have children predict what this fictional story will be about and then read to see whether their predictions were correct.

After Reading the Selection, page 103

 ASSESS Comprehension Check

1. (**Recognizing Setting**) Have children tell where Bat was when he talked to Eagle. Then have them tell where he went next. A
2. (**Drawing Conclusions**) Ask children to review Bat's words and actions in the story. G
3. (**Sequencing**) Invite a volunteer to describe what Bat was doing when Eagle flew by. A
4. (**Understanding Realism and Fantasy**) Have children discuss which story events could happen in real life and which could not. F
5. (**Recognizing Setting**) Possible response: In the beginning of the story, Bat lives in the sky. At the end of the story, Bat lives in a cave.
6. (**Understanding Realism and Fantasy**) Possible response: A bat could fly in the sky.

MEETING INDIVIDUAL NEEDS/ESL

To help children recognize the story settings, have each child draw a picture of a setting that is described in the story, including details that show where and when that part of the story took place. Children can also write or dictate captions to go with their picture. Invite children to share their drawings with one another and read their captions aloud.

Student Book pages 104–105

Save the Trees!

SYNOPSIS

This is the true story of Julia Hill, a woman who lived in a redwood tree for two years to spread the message that saving trees is very important.

GENRE: Nonfiction (Social Studies Article)

Remind children that a nonfiction article gives facts about a particular topic.

COMPREHENSION FOCUS SKILLS

Identifying Cause and Effect

Identifying Fact and Opinion

Sequencing

Drawing Conclusions

Reviewing the Comprehension Skills

Review the following comprehension skills, which are presented in this article.

- **Identifying Cause and Effect:** The cause is why something happens. An effect is what happens because of it.
- **Identifying Fact and Opinion:** A fact is something that can be proven. An opinion is what one person thinks or believes.
- **Sequencing:** Sequence is the order in which events happen.
- **Drawing Conclusions:** Authors do not always tell you everything. Sometimes you must use clues from the story, along with what you already know, to draw conclusions.

Reading the Selection, page 104

⭐ Get Ready to Read

Have children set purposes for reading. Ask them to read the title of the article and describe what they see in the photographs. Then have them predict what this article will be about. Ask children to read to see whether their predictions were correct.

After Reading the Selection, page 105

ASSESS Comprehension Check

1. **(Identifying Cause and Effect)** Have children explain, in their own words, why Julia Hill climbed the tree. A
2. **(Identifying Fact and Opinion)** Have children read each answer choice and ask themselves, "Can this be proven true?" F
3. **(Identifying Cause and Effect)** Ask children to tell what happened right before Julia climbed down from the tree. B
4. **(Identifying Fact and Opinion)** Invite volunteers to share some facts mentioned in the article. F
5. **(Sequencing)** Julia Hill climbed down from her tree.
6. **(Drawing Conclusions)** Possible response: It would be hard to be away from friends and family for two years.

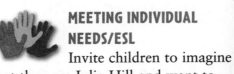

MEETING INDIVIDUAL NEEDS/ESL

Invite children to imagine that they are Julia Hill and want to explain to people why they climbed the tree. Then work with small groups of children to rewrite the article from Julia's point of view, having children dictate statements of fact and Julia's opinion for you to record. Read aloud the completed article.

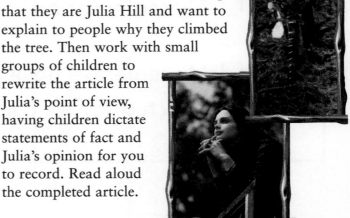

Writing Sentences About a Dog or a Cat

Use the checklist below as a guide as you write. To get the highest score, be sure you have checked each box.

First write a draft. Then check it against the checklist. Use the checklist to see how to make your work better. Then change your writing as needed.

For a Score of 4

☐ My sentences tell about a dog or a cat.

☐ One sentence has a main idea.

☐ Two other sentences give details that support the main idea.

☐ My sentences are clear and easy to read.

☐ My sentences have no mistakes in grammar, punctuation, or capitalization.

Name _____

Writing a Summary About a Toy

Use the checklist below as a guide as you write. To get the highest score, be sure you have checked each box.

First write a draft. Then check it against the checklist. Use the checklist to see how to make your work better. Then change your writing as needed.

For a Score of 4

☐ My summary tells about a toy.

☐ My summary has two sentences.

☐ The sentences tell important ideas about what the toy is like.

☐ My sentences are clear and easy to read.

☐ My summary has no mistakes in grammar, punctuation, or capitalization.

Name _____

Writing a Story About a Pet

Use the checklist below as a guide as you write. To get the highest score, be sure you have checked each box.

First write a draft. Then check it against the checklist. Use the checklist to see how to make your work better. Then change your writing as needed.

For a Score of 4

☐ My story is about a pet I would like to have.

☐ My story has a clear beginning, middle, and end.

☐ The events in my story could happen in real life.

☐ My story tells about the events in the order in which they happen.

☐ My story has no mistakes in grammar, punctuation, or capitalization.

© Steck-Vaughn Company

Name _____

Writing Sentences About an Animal I Like

Use the checklist below as a guide as you write. To get the highest score, be sure you have checked each box.

First write a draft. Then check it against the checklist. Use the checklist to see how to make your work better. Then change your writing as needed.

For a Score of 4

☐ My sentences explain why people should like a certain animal.

☐ I have included three or more details that will make others feel the same way I do about the animal.

☐ My sentences are clear and easy to read.

☐ My sentences have no mistakes in grammar, punctuation, or capitalization.

Name _____

Writing Sentences About What Might Happen

Use the checklist below as a guide as you write. To get the highest score, be sure you have checked each box.

First write a draft. Then check it against the checklist. Use the checklist to see how to make your work better. Then change your writing as needed.

For a Score of 4

☐ My sentences tell what the cat does next or what happens to the cat because of what it does.

☐ My sentences give details about why the cat acts as it does.

☐ My sentences are clear and easy to read.

☐ My sentences have no mistakes in grammar, punctuation, or capitalization.

Name _____

Writing Sentences That Compare and Contrast

Use the checklist below as a guide as you write. To get the highest score, be sure you have checked each box.

First write a draft. Then check it against the checklist. Use the checklist to see how to make your work better. Then change your writing as needed.

For a Score of 4

☐ My sentences explain at least two ways the animals are alike and at least two ways the animals are different.

☐ I have included more than one clue word that compares or contrasts.

☐ The facts are clear and easy to read.

☐ My sentences have no mistakes in grammar, punctuation, or capitalization.

Name _____

Writing Sentences About a Place in the Afternoon

Use the checklist below as a guide as you write. To get the highest score, be sure you have checked each box.

First write a draft. Then check it against the checklist. Use the checklist to see how to make your work better. Then change your writing as needed.

For a Score of 4

☐ My sentences describe a trail, park, or playground in the afternoon.

☐ I have included two or more details that tell about the time and the place.

☐ My sentences are clear and easy to read.

☐ My sentences have no mistakes in grammar, punctuation, or capitalization.

Name _____

Writing Fact and Opinion Sentences

Use the checklist below as a guide as you write. To get the highest score, be sure you have checked each box.

First write a draft. Then check it against the checklist. Use the checklist to see how to make your work better. Then change your writing as needed.

For a Score of 4

☐ My sentences tell about an animal that I know about.

☐ I have included two or more facts about the animal.

☐ I have included two or more opinions about the animal.

☐ My sentences are clear and easy to read.

☐ My sentences have no mistakes in grammar, punctuation, or capitalization.

Name _____

Writing a Fantasy Story About Yourself

Use the checklist below as a guide as you write. To get the highest score, be sure you have checked each box.

First write a draft. Then check it against the checklist. Use the checklist to see how to make your work better. Then change your writing as needed.

For a Score of 4

☐ My story is a fantasy about myself.

☐ I have included three or more things I could not really do.

☐ My story has a clear beginning, middle, and end.

☐ My story's plot is clear and easy to read.

☐ My story has no mistakes in grammar, punctuation, or capitalization.

Name _____

Writing Cause and Effect Sentences

Use the checklist below as a guide as you write. To get the highest score, be sure you have checked each box.

First write a draft. Then check it against the checklist. Use the checklist to see how to make your work better. Then change your writing as needed.

For a Score of 4

☐ My sentences are about a time when I did well in a school activity or playing a sport.

☐ My sentences include one or two causes that tell why I did well.

☐ My sentences include one or two effects that tell what happened.

☐ My sentences have no mistakes in grammar, punctuation, or capitalization.

Name _____

Writing Mystery Sentences

Use the checklist below as a guide as you write. To get the highest score, be sure you have checked each box.

First write a draft. Then check it against the checklist. Use the checklist to see how to make your work better. Then change your writing as needed.

For a Score of 4

☐ My sentences tell about a time when I lost something and then found it.

☐ I have included three or more clues that I used to find the missing object.

☐ I have described what I thought happened to the object and what really happened in the end.

☐ My sentences have no mistakes in grammar, punctuation, or capitalization.

Name _____

Writing About How To Do Something

Use the checklist below as a guide as you write. To get the highest score, be sure you have checked each box.

First write a draft. Then check it against the checklist. Use the checklist to see how to make your work better. Then change your writing as needed.

For a Score of 4

- ☐ My writing has three or four sentences about something I can do.

- ☐ My sentences tell the steps I take to do it.

- ☐ The steps are in order.

- ☐ Each step includes clue words to show the order of events.

- ☐ My sentences have no mistakes in grammar, punctuation, or capitalization.

Name _____

Dear Family of _____,

Your child is reading stories that help with learning to understand what he or she reads. Here are some things you can do with your child to help at home.

- Get a library card for your child. Make regular trips to your local library and ask your child to pick out a book each time you visit. Discuss the book your child is reading. Ask him or her to tell you about the book and give his or her ideas about it.

- Set aside a time for reading at home. It could be before bed, on a Sunday night, or whenever you and your child like. You may even ask your child to read to a younger family member.

- Try to read articles from newspapers or magazines to your child often. Talk about the main idea of the article. Underline some of the words your child doesn't know, and find their meanings in a dictionary.

- Help your child write in a journal. Suggest that he or she start by simply telling what happens in his or her life each day. You might give your child a notebook to make it special.

Estimada familia de _____,

Su niño/a está leyendo historias y artículos que ayudan a que aprenda a entender lo que él o ella lee. Aquí hay algunas cosas que puede hacer en casa con su niño/a.

- Adquiera una tarjeta de la biblioteca para su niño/a. Haga viajes frecuentes a su biblioteca más cercana y pregúntele a su niño/a que escoja un libro en cada visita. Platiquen del libro que su niño/a está leyendo. Cuando su niño/a haya terminado el libro, pregúntele acerca del libro y que le comente sus ideas sobre él.

- Aparte un tiempo para leer en casa. Puede ser antes de acostarse, en domingo por la noche, o cuando ustedes quieran. Incluso puede preguntarle a su niño/a que le lea a un miembro de la familia más pequeño.

- Trate seguido de leer con su niño/a algunos de los artículos de periódicos ó revistas . Platiquen sobre la idea principal del artículo. Subraye palabras que su niño/a no conozca y busquen su significado en un diccionario.

- Ayude que su niño/a escriba un diario. Sugiera que simplemente escriba lo que pasa en su vida cada día. Podría darle a su niño/a un cuaderno para hacerlo más especial.

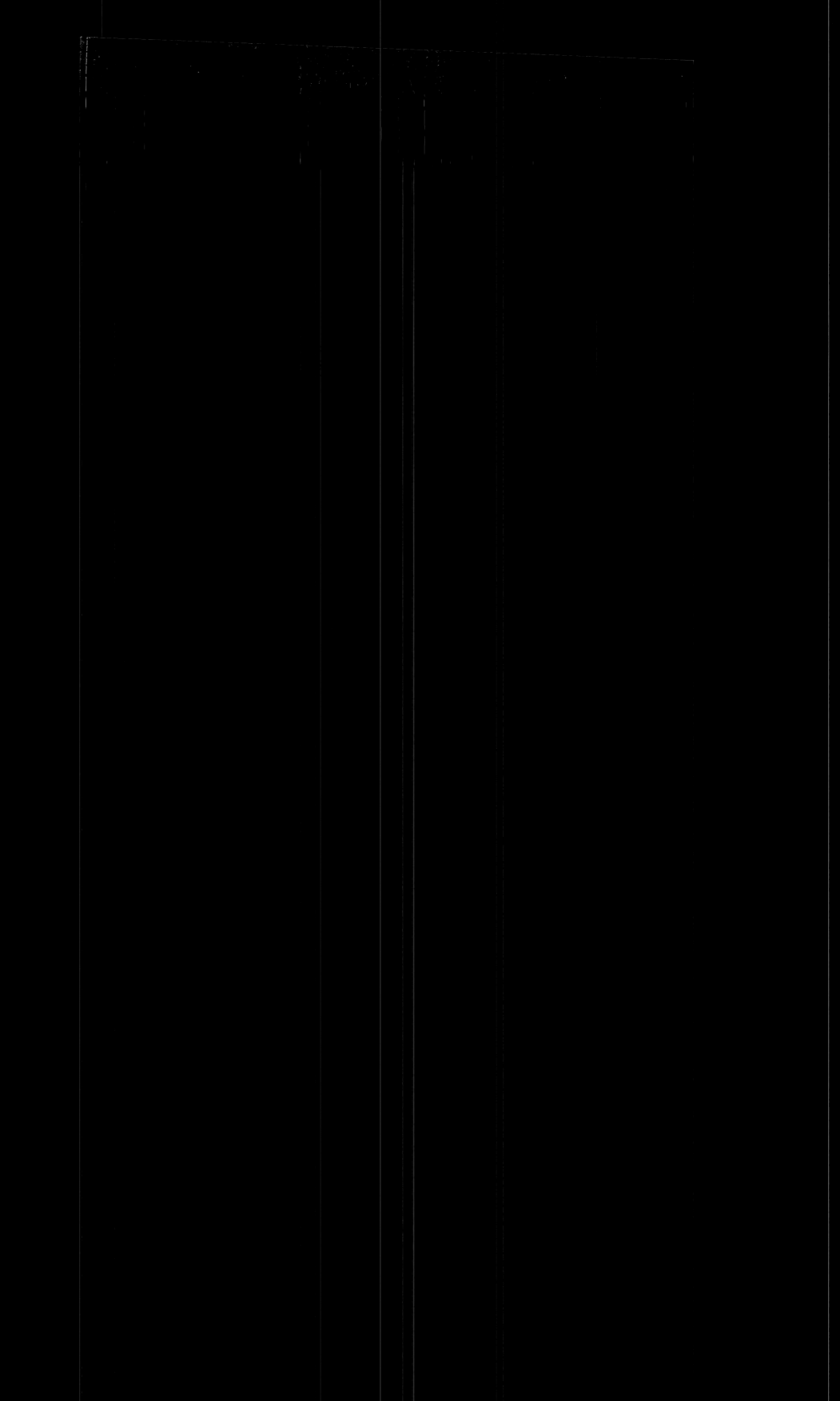

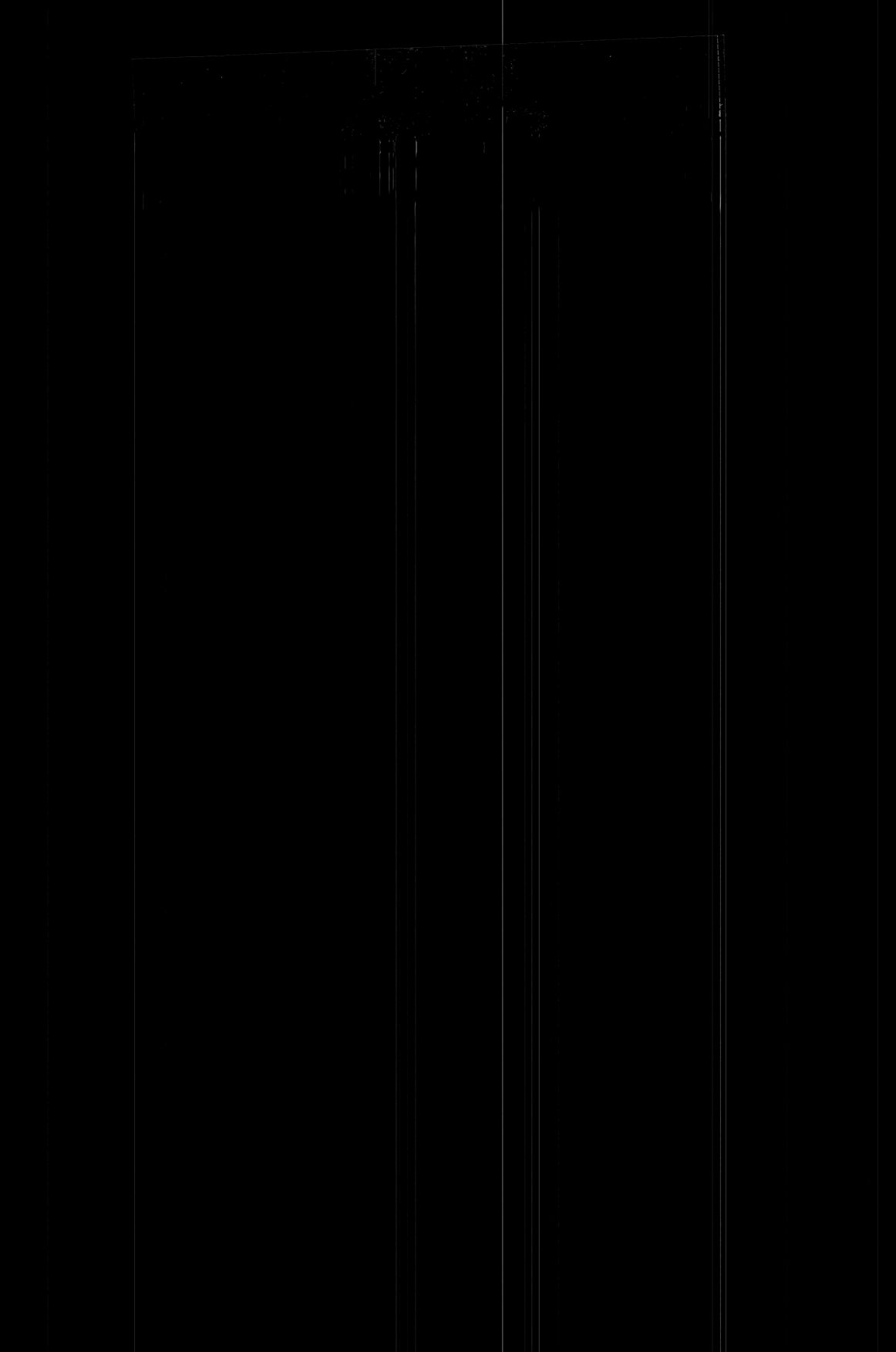

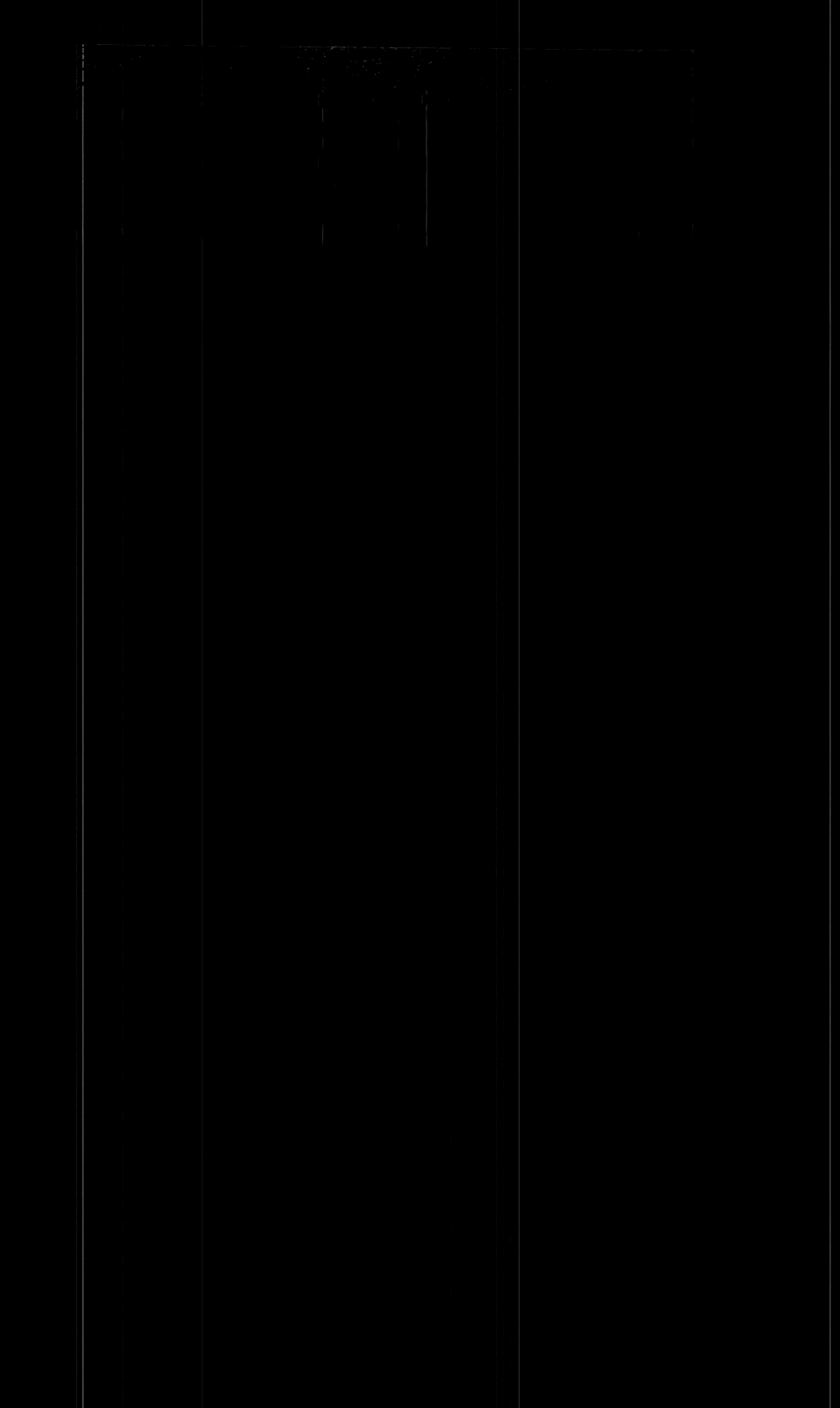

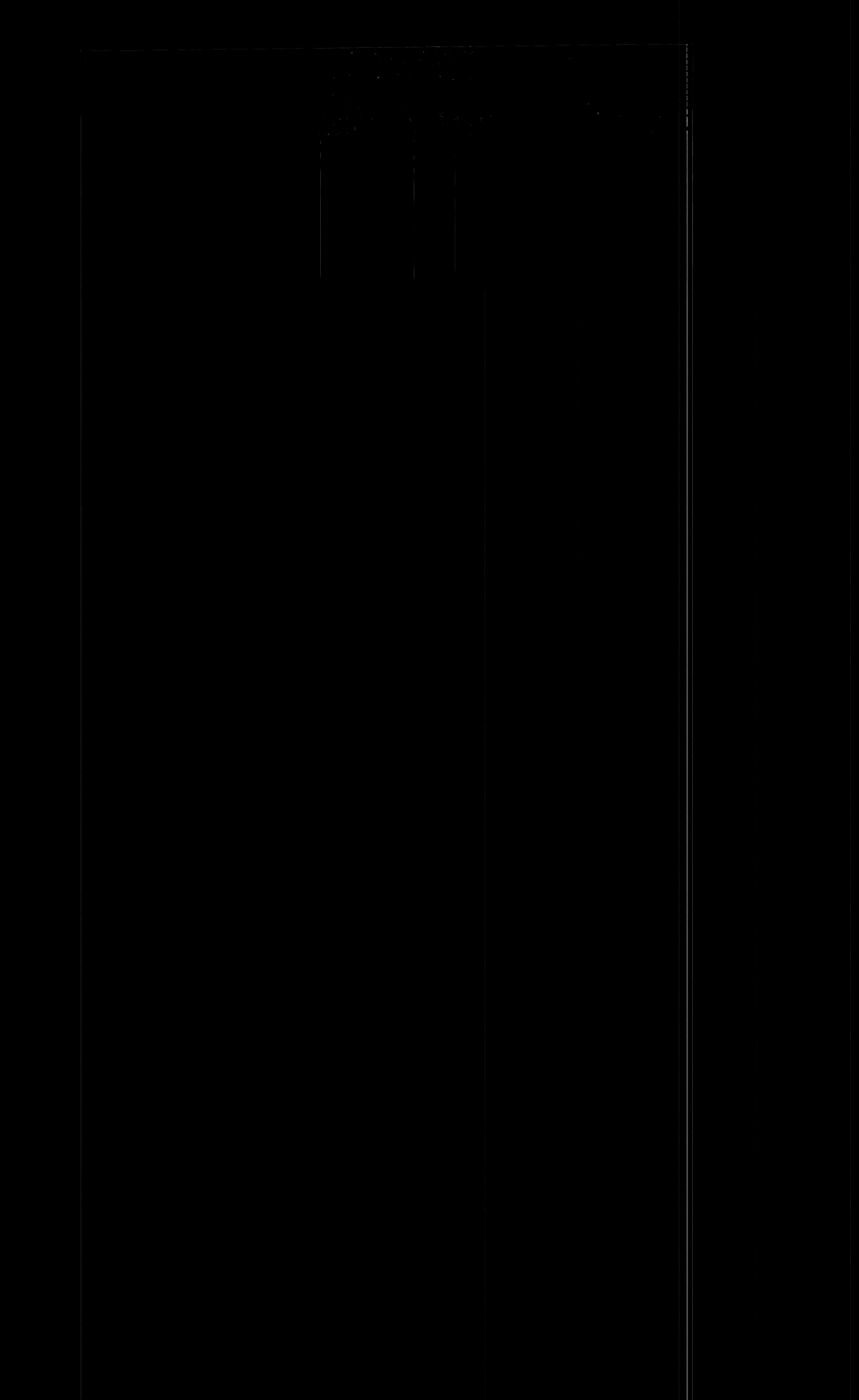

Writing Sentences That Compare and Contrast

Use the checklist below as a guide as you write. To get the highest score, be sure you have checked each box.

First write a draft. Then check it against the checklist. Use the checklist to see how to make your work better. Then change your writing as needed.

For a Score of 4

☐ My sentences explain at least two ways the animals are alike and at least two ways the animals are different.

☐ I have included more than one clue word that compares or contrasts.

☐ The facts are clear and easy to read.

☐ My sentences have no mistakes in grammar, punctuation, or capitalization.

Name _____

Writing Mystery Sentences

Use the checklist below as a guide as you write. To get the highest score, be sure you have checked each box.

First write a draft. Then check it against the checklist. Use the checklist to see how to make your work better. Then change your writing as needed.

For a Score of 4

☐ My sentences tell about a time when I lost something and then found it.

☐ I have included three or more clues that I used to find the missing object.

☐ I have described what I thought happened to the object and what really happened in the end.

☐ My sentences have no mistakes in grammar, punctuation, or capitalization.

Name _____

Writing About How To Do Something

Use the checklist below as a guide as you write. To get the highest score, be sure you have checked each box.

First write a draft. Then check it against the checklist. Use the checklist to see how to make your work better. Then change your writing as needed.

For a Score of 4

☐ My writing has three or four sentences about something I can do.

☐ My sentences tell the steps I take to do it.

☐ The steps are in order.

☐ Each step includes clue words to show the order of events.

☐ My sentences have no mistakes in grammar, punctuation, or capitalization.

Name _____

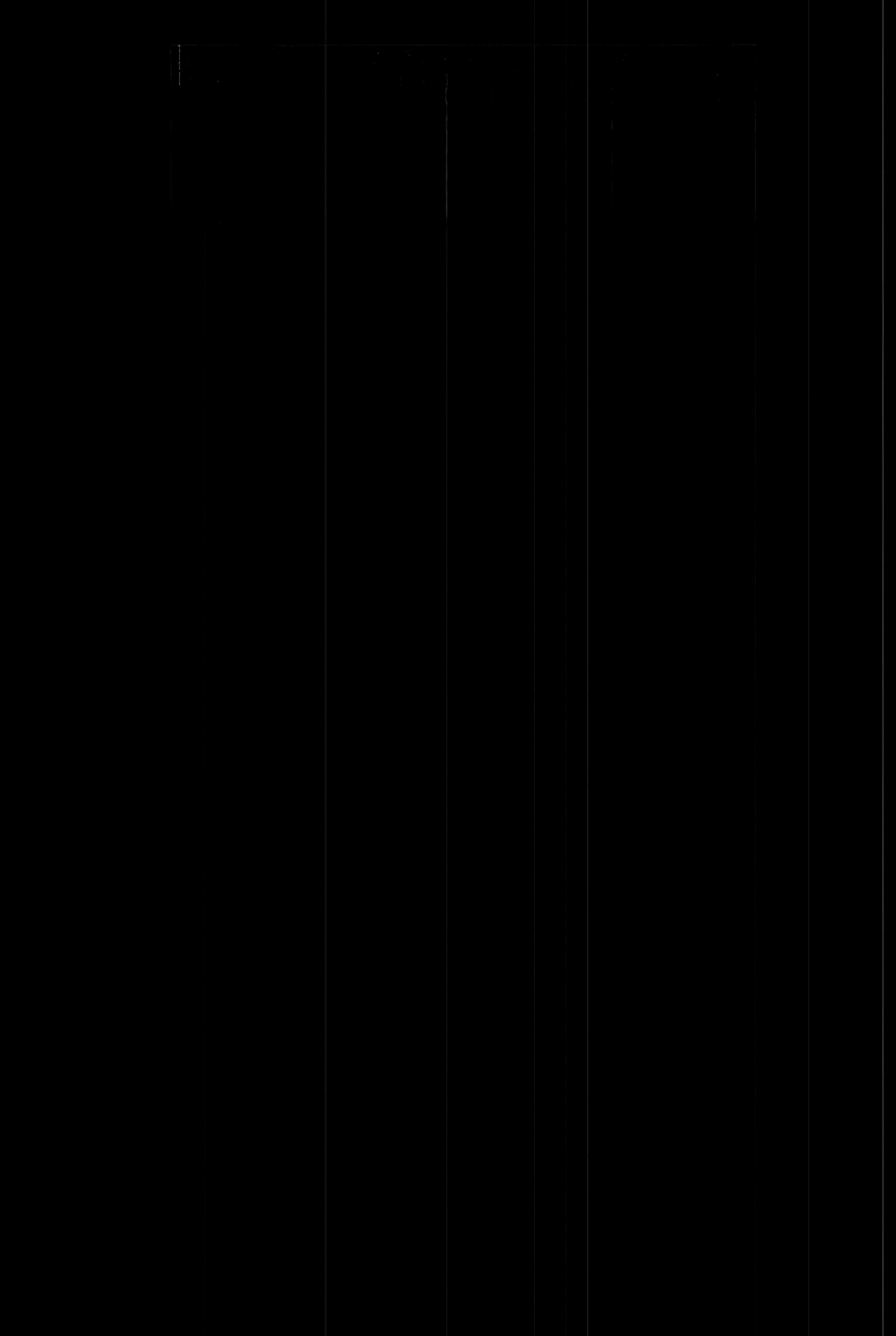